ART and BEAUTY

by MAURICE DE WULF

Translated by

SISTER MARY GONZAGA UDELL, O.P.

AQUINAS COLLEGE
GRAND RAPIDS, MICHIGAN

B. HERDER BOOK CO.

15 & 17 SOUTH BROADWAY, ST. LOUIS 2, MO.
AND
33 QUEEN SQUARE, LONDON, W. C.
1950

NIHIL OBSTAT

Wm. Fischer, S.T.D.

Censor Librorum

IMPRIMATUR

✠ *Joseph E. Ritter*

Archiepiscopus

Sti. Ludovici, die 8a Novembris, 1950

Vail-Ballou Press, Inc., Binghamton and New York

SEP 4

Translator's Preface

MAURICE DE WULF was well known to the learned public. Author of some twenty-five publications, professor of philosophy at Louvain University since 1893, visiting lecturer at Harvard in the year 1915–1916, and again in 1920, and professor of philosophy at the same university from 1921 to 1928, he was long looked upon as one of the leading figures in the revival of Scholasticism, as well as its more articulate exponent. The lectures here given in translation were delivered and published shortly after World War I and revised in 1943. De Wulf was a Thomistic Scholastic and as such displayed in his writings something of the perennial quality characteristic of Aquinas. The utterances of such a thinker have ever about them the newness and freshness of truth itself.

The subject discussed here is not one that has received sufficient attention at the hands of scholastic writers. In fact a fully rounded theory of beauty remains still to be developed in the scholastic field. Idealistic philosophers, tinctured deep with Kantianism and Hegelianism, have been the most prolific promoters of pure subjectivism as the essence of the aesthetic experience. It was this extreme position that Professor De Wulf felt called upon to refute. Though the emphasis would be shifted today from the effort to dislodge erroneous theories to the attempt at explicit definition of beauty and its human appeal, no statement contained in these lectures can be completely gainsaid. Neither should any be disregarded.

And if this translation had no other purpose than the advancement of knowledge one short step along the route of scholastic theory of aesthetic in the making, it would be of supreme value to the student of a philosophy of beauty. But he will find it far more than this. Nearly all the elements for a complete explanation of the appeal of the beautiful are here. The translator offers the work with the conviction that it will be received with gratitude by teachers and pupils alike wherever the serious attempt is being made to develop a valid aesthetics.

SISTER M. GONZAGA UDELL, O.P.

Author's Preface

THE studies contained in this volume are presented in the form of conferences, a form they received when, as a member of the Faculty of Letters of Poitiers, I was given the honor by the Minister of Public Instruction of France of delivering a series of public lectures on philosophy.

Being a sort of collaboration with the general public, the studies possess a highly popular character; the understanding of them does not require professional training in philosophy: they do, however, presuppose a philosophic system, especially a psychology and a metaphysics of which the informed reader will easily recognize the essential characteristics. The groundwork and building stones which make up the regular course of this philosophy of art are Greek doctrines, principally Aristotelian, and medieval. But the edifice is not a simple historic reconstruction, for the borrowings made from the past are thrown into the mold of contemporary thought. We have tried to present in an interesting way the fundamental principles of Aristotle and St. Thomas.

No one, then, will be surprised that we attempt to establish a philosophy of art which is of a character both intellectual and objective. At first sight it may appear that, because of this twofold tendency, our theory is at variance with contemporary ideas. On closer examination, however, the reader will see that the tendency is in the opposite direction, a closer approach to present-day thought rather than a departure from it. In reality, at present a reaction is evident on all sides against an excess of subjectivism; and intellectual knowledge, having been long denied all place in the aesthetic experience, now resumes triumphantly the place that rightly belongs to it. To admit that there exists a world other than that of our subjective states is to subscribe to an interpretation more in keeping with the real, and thus also with artistic reality. To establish the theory that this extramental world is accessible through multiple activities of the conscious ego, and that by these modes of activity the intellective process based on abstraction occupies a place, is to construct a psychology more adequate and thus more human.

The intellectual and objective philosophy to which we appeal in order to interpret the beauty of art will not, therefore, be an intrusion, if it guards against all exclusiveness and does not itself compromise that which gives it its value. As all the functions of the conscious being, intellectual and otherwise, contribute to the comprehension of a work of art, the intellective factor is not sufficient to explain the harmonious unity of the artistic impression. On the other hand, beauty is not a purely objective attribute, a simple manner of the work of art; for this attribute, this manner of being, is strictly dependent on the psychological process; subjectivism and objectivism are mutually complementary, and intellectualism is strengthened by the doctrines which have striven to smother it. Once more the truth is a happy medium, this happy medium difficult of retention by the human mind, which tends ever to oscillate from one extreme to the other, like the beam of a balance. The theory of the law of averages, so conformable to the genius of Aristotle, so thoroughly in keeping with human nature, again resumes its rights.

The general character that we have wished to preserve in these lectures explains why technical terminology is reduced to a minimum and historical ideas are rare.

Three lectures on the aesthetics of the thirteenth century published in an appendix will permit the reader to see to what a degree certain medieval doctrines have been utilized in this work

MAURICE DE WULF

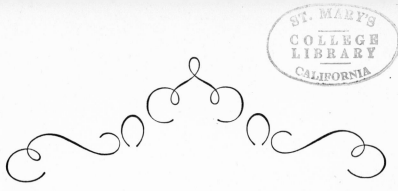

Contents

CHAPTER I

Ideas and Method

IMPRESSION OF ART

THE ideas that form the starting point for the launching of a course of instruction in any branch of knowledge are necessarily merely provisional for the understanding of its scope and are not intended to be its perfect and adequate presentation. They may be compared to the blossoms and flowers that make way for the fruit, since they indicate the terminals or limits which are the outcome of a patient study.

Imperfect though they are, these first notions easily justify their presence by furnishing matter for contrast: to know what a thing is not is a step toward an understanding of what it is. To know what does not constitute a philosophy of art is to mark, to some degree, the boundaries of the subject; to point out its distinguishing features from closely related disciplines, and to indicate its general contours in the terrain

I

which it embraces. In such a way does the traveler in a strange country proceed. He sets the approximate limits of his tour: the plateaus, for instance, of Central France,—Touraine, Poitou, Brittany—and thereby plans to forego at the outset the view of such or such another city, of such or such a point of interest, situated outside the line of travel decided upon. This constitutes the first general plan of procedure, negative if you will, but one which will be followed by the positive and carefully selected stages of the journey.

At the entrance upon our study it is wise to show that the philosophy of art is a different thing from the criticism of works of art or from the history of art, subjects with which it is often confounded; and these three disciplines of the mind are in their turn to be distinguished from the impression of art, the object of the study of all three from various points of view.

The impression of art is that delightful stirring of the emotions which is produced in us when we are in contact with an artistic production. The nature of this impression we shall consider later on.

By the term "artist" we must understand both the one who produces the work and the one who enjoys a production done by another. The artist is absorbed in the work he contemplates. By a sort of aesthetic shock it takes possession of all the activities of his conscious being,—senses, imagination, intellect, emotions, loves—all the energies converging toward a kind of intuition and becoming centered in it; and the soul is plunged into an intoxication comparable to nothing else.

Whether we contemplate the form of a monument, the pose of a statue, the episodes of a drama, the motif of a painting, the evolution of a musical theme, this taking possession is spontaneous and direct, and does not imply reflective judgment on the value of the work.

Is it to be understood, then, that we do not reflect in the presence of a work of art or that we refrain from passing judgment? No. Reflection and cool discrimination are not slow to intrude themselves, so much the more imperiously as the mind is more cultivated. But through their intervention they break the first charm, and then the enjoyment of the art gives place to criticism.

To criticize (from the Greek κρίνειν, to discern) is to reflect, that is, to make a return of the mind (reflect), a folding back upon a state of consciousness, and to pass a judgment by reason of this return. The art critic directs his attention to the technical procedures the artist used and pronounces on their value. What does this work entail; what are its requirements?

Let us limit ourselves to noting three of its main characteristics: each art has its own proper standards of criticism; so, too, has each work of art; and this criticism presupposes the enjoyment of the art and is capable of alternating with that enjoyment.

First, since each art has its technique, its means of expression, and its method of procedure imposed upon it by the matter put into the work, each has also its own norm of judgment. Musical criticism, for example, judges the workmanship of the themes and their combination; criticism of

theatrical art concerns itself with imitations, postures, scenery, and adaptation of the vocal expression to the action of the scene; literary criticism appraises ideas and the language in which they are expressed.

Hence the critic of any art, called upon to judge the quality of a work, ought to possess the general technique of the art which he judges and take into account the personal applications an artist makes of them in a given case. The more thoroughly he investigates the latter's artistic resources, the better also he will make comprehensible to ordinary people, who are not professionals but merely persons of good taste, how to appreciate the work of painters or sculptors, musicians or architects, novelists or dramatists. In the studies of a Fromentin, of a Jules Lemaître, of a Camille Bellaigue, of a Violet-le-Duc, we discern at once a man initiated into the requirements of excellence in painting, in literature, in music, or in architecture.

And this is not all. Not only does criticism vary from one art to another, but even from one work to another in the same art. It does not consist of a series of rules or of prescriptions such as we find in the poetic art of Horace or of Boileau; this art is as individual as the work of art itself, or of a group of works, the fruit of one artistic career, or even of a school. Rubens ought not to be brought under the same judgment as Rembrandt since each understood differently the technique of the palette. Read, if you wish to be convinced of this, the incomparable pages that Fromentin has written on the masters of former times. This book is rich in instructive contents. We meet here well-developed analyses of the means and methods of the great painter of Antwerp, of the astonishing account to which he was able to turn the most unlikely colors and a few simple formulas, and of his style so elementary that it seemed to the author that a school-boy would be able to follow it. And yet it had no imitators; "this point so unfathomable, so incomprehensible, this irreducible atom, this nothing which among all the things of this world is called inspiration, grace, or gift, and which is everything." [1]

A genuine enthusiasm pervades this book: the reader feels that the author has spent long hours in converse with the canvases which he analyses, that before being a critic of art he was first an artist himself, and that in the very course of his reflections and judgments the artist, for moments at a time, has imposed silence on the critic and has abandoned himself by recollection to the charm of a direct and spontaneous enjoyment. "Do you wish us to return to the picture again for a moment?" writes Fromentin on the subject of Rubens' *Miraculous Draught of Fishes*. "It is there at hand. This is an occasion that does not come to one often and which I shall not have again: I seize it." This example gives us a vivid realization of one last point: a true criticism of art can alternate with its impression; and the state of reflective study with spontaneous enjoyment.

What Fromentin says of the alternation of aesthetic delight with the study of artistic procedure has been experienced by all of us. Nearly everyone, in the course of listening to a

[1] *Les maîtres d'autrefois* (Paris, 1876), p. 58.

musical production, of a visit to a church, of the contemplation of a picture, has sought for that which, in a given technique, had the power to please him; after several moments he was ready to bring this sort of parenthesis to a close and to return to the direct contact with the beloved work. The enjoyment of art leads the man of culture instinctively to an analysis of the procedures used in the artistic production; in its turn, this analysis brings the soul back to complete abandonment, to the delectable influence of the artistic impression.

Artistic criticism is closely allied to the history of art. The artist is not a superhuman being, free from the influence of his environment and unaffected by the achievements of his forebears. We would be wrong in considering him in the light of a miraculous flower whose origin and development had escaped the ordinary laws of generation and growth. Homer or Virgil, Rubens or Raphael, Beethoven or Wagner, each is a product of his times, and it is necessary to put him back there in order to understand his true physiognomy. Art, as all other manifestations of psychic life, has a tradition, which, like a chain of gold, binds together men and schools. The history of art establishes these connections and dependences. Undoubtedly it leaves to archaeology to decide the philological documentation of the productions of the past, to interpret their spirit, and to follow the evolution of artistic skills; but it is no less true that more and more art criticism is drawn along in the wake of history. It assays a picture of "the evolution of the forms and of the life of artistic monuments." [2]

[2] Michel, *Histoire de l'art,* I, iii.

Criticism and the history of art are not the only points of view which a person may take in the study of a work of art; neither of them is identified with philosophy. If an encyclopedia should assemble criticisms of all the works of art of the past and of the present, and these followed by a history of art, such a work could not be called a philosophy. You would have there a vast stock of material from which to formulate a philosophy of art, but this task itself would still remain to be done.

THE PHILOSOPHY OF ART

The philosophy of art is distinct from a criticism of art and also from its history. The following illustrations will make this fact clear.

The beautiful church of Notre Dame la Grande, whose graceful tower rises above the small radiating apses, is not a mere assemblage of pillars and columns, of arches and galleries. The structure forms an organic whole, its thousand details woven into a unity. One of the most powerful means by which this unity is realized is the rounded arch occurring again and again along with the other architectural motifs which are the function of the vaultings of the Roman vault. Suppose for a moment that by an awkward restoration the vaultings of the central nave should be pulled down and then replaced by crossed pointed arches; the harmony of lines and style of the building would be compromised. This is the unsatisfactory impression which remains after a visit to the cathedral of Cordova, a superb and colossal mosque, where the "horseshoe arch" should have remained the organic and sovereign form, but inside which has been carved a veritable Gothic church. In fact, there is no longer present one monument; there are two, one inserted in the other to the disfigurement of both. To realize how such architectural incongruities reduce the artistic value of a work you need not be a great savant in the matter of art.

Why must there be unity in an edifice and, in general, in every work that aspires to be beautiful? What does unity mean in a work of art? What is its aesthetic function? Here we have an inquiry pertaining to a criticism neither of architecture nor of art, but to philosophy.

Another example: Art penetrates into all the domains of modern industry; it embellishes the façades of our houses and the furniture; it bestows a smile upon the familiar objects of our lives. The alignment of our streets, the choice of sites of public buildings, the structural form of schools, railway stations, banks, all come under art's royal sway. Now, the beauty of a house is not independent of its fitness as a place to live in. No one would find it beautiful if the architect—I take an extreme case—should forget to put in a stairway from the first to the second floor. A chair will not be beautiful, whatever its price or its decoration, if the seat is too narrow to be sat on. A railway station will not be beautiful, however rich its architecture, if it is ill adapted to the coming and going of trains and of travelers. Once again we have a case of the elementary criticism of art. But in these various instances do we not always make an appeal to the purpose of the object, to its utility? Then has utility a value in the artistic impression? As far as an object appears to be useful does it not cease to be beautiful? Again, the answer to this question does not lie in the realm of the criticism of art, but in that of philosophy. We shall return to this subject later on.

Thus it can be seen that the philosophy of art is a study of another order. It rises above all kinds of technique and of criticism; it is not attached to the study of an individual work but dominates them all. It is placed at the summit of a pyramid, the base of which would be occupied by art criticism, and the central part by the history of art. It is of a nature to be applicable to works of art at any moment of time and in any environment in which they appear, for it has for its object the study of the factors which in any work constitute the essence of beauty. Philosophy of art is concerned with problems of a general character since these are presented in regard to all works of art; and because of this general character the study which now interests us belongs in the class of philosophical science. What does this statement mean?

THE PHILOSOPHICAL CYCLE

This is not the place to define philosophy or to determine its relations with the various other sciences.[3] One statement by way of comparison will suffice. The foreigner who would wish to know all Paris would visit it quarter by quarter, monuments and museums, palaces and public places, boulevards and gardens. But even though he would have had the

---

[3] See De Wulf, *Initiation à la philosophie thomiste* (Louvain, 1932), chap. 2.

leisure to become acquainted in detail with the riches of the
great city, there would remain a second way of knowing it.
From the summit of the Eiffel Tower, from the basket of a
balloon or the seat of an airplane, the metropolis would take
on a totally new aspect. This would reveal, instead, its general
structure, the coordination of the great boulevards, the
meanderings of the Seine, the forms and respective positions
of the monuments, all things which the traveler would not
have been able to learn in the course of his successive excur-
sions.

And thus it is with the world we inhabit. The particular
sciences concern themselves each with a special aspect
thereof, as each entrenches itself in a corner of reality. Thus
chemistry investigates the composition and decomposition of
matter; civil law, the juridical relations among citizens; but
chemistry remains as much a stranger to the theory of con-
tracts as does civil law to the composition of chlorine.

Now in contrast to this parceled-out study of the universe,
there is a method by which it may be viewed in its entirety,
in the totality of the profoundest principles to be found in all
things. This method is that of philosophy. The man of
science inspects the world in detail; the philosopher contemplates it from the vantage of a belvedere; he sees large and
wide, makes syntheses, and arrives at unity.

What are these fundamental principles that are found in
all reality, these points of view that dominate all? Here is the
answer which was given by Aristotle and after him by the
principal philosophers of the Arabian and Western Middle

Ages. These are, on the one hand, aspects of reality which affect every sensible being (theoretic philosophy); on the other hand, they are functions by which man enters into relation with that reality (practical philosophy).

Certain aspects affect the totality of the sensible things of the universe; we find them everywhere; they are outside us [4] since we project our mental activity beyond ourselves to consider them. (The word "consider" gives the name to theoretic philosophy from the Greek word θεωρεῖν, meaning "to consider that which is"). These aspects are the foundation for the division of theoretic philosophy into three branches: change and development, comprising the whole sensible universe including man (physics and psychology); quantity (mathematics); and lastly, being itself with its general attributes of unity, goodness, causality, and order (metaphysics).

As distinguished from theoretical philosophy stands that which is practical or normative: this is the study of the life of relations which man entertains with the real and of which he himself is the artisan (hence the name "practical" from πράττειν). It is subdivided according to three great functions proper to man in governing these relations; knowing, willing, and producing. There is nothing which man cannot know after a fashion, no matter how imperfect that knowledge may be. Logic indicates the laws according to which he arranges his knowledge in the various sciences. There is nothing good which he cannot will and which cannot become matter for

[4] Thomas Aquinas, *In X Lib. ad Nicom.*, Bk. I, 1, i.

morality; moral law governs his conduct. Man's exterior productions have no limit. The philosophy of art determines how, under the direction of reason, these works may become manifest, clothed in the radiance of beauty.

It is interesting to note how the character of generality in the philosophy of art magnifies human art. Every outward production of man has the power to cover itself with the aesthetic imprint, making the domain of art as vast as reality itself.[5]

HARMONY OF BRANCHES OF PHILOSOPHY

The foregoing considerations bring in as a corollary a second characteristic of the philosophy of art: it has the solidarity of a doctrinal code. The philosophy of art of a Plato could not resemble that of a Dante, nor the aesthetic of Schopenhauer that of Herbert Spencer, any more than the tower of a Gothic church could resemble the minaret of a mosque. Plato says the work of art is "a shadow of a shadow";

[5] The Aristotelian and medieval classification speaks of the philosophy of arts and not of the philosophy of art. In assigning to the latter the place occupied by the philosophy of the arts in the trilogy of philosophical sciences, we merely extend its application to the scope already therein implied. The philosophy of art occupies a different place in the philosophical cycle as arranged by modern thinkers. In their scheme (according to Wolf) the classification of the philosophic sciences retains, from the Middle Ages, the division of philosophy into the theoretic and the practical, but divides each of these again according to new principles. Theoretic philosophy comprises general and special metaphysics, the latter subdividing into cosmology, psychology, and theodicy; practical philosophy embraces ethics, economics, and politics. Furthermore, logic is regarded as a preparatory science to all the other branches of philosophy. It was a disciple of Leibnitz, Alfred Baumgarten, who found a special place in this synthesis for aesthetics, or the philosophic study of beauty and of art.

Dante calls it the "grandson of God"; Schopenhauer compares it to an intoxicating drink which makes one forget for the moment the woes of life; Herbert Spencer sees in it the overcharge of a too full activity. Behold so many irreducible notions. To try to reduce these to a unity would be as utopian as to attempt to form a single being by clamping together parts borrowed from different kinds of organisms. Nature does not graft the head of a horse on a human trunk, and the rose bush does not adorn itself with sprays of violets. In the same way in philosophy everything takes its place in organic unity; the science forms a systematic whole.

The philosophy of art does not move in the void. At each step it makes its borrowings from psychology, or its snatches from metaphysics; it enters into relations with morality and civil law when bearing witness to the events of the present hour; it clings to the fringes of every field of speculative thought. And for this reason all the controversies of philosophers have their echoes in the philosophy of art. Here lies the deep reason why it is not sufficient for him who wishes to take it up to be a prolific writer or a critic of art. More than once along our route we shall hear the echoes of great philosophical doctrines clashing in the arena of today.

AUXILIARY SUBJECTS

As physical and chemical sciences furnish a point of departure for cosmology, or for the philosophic study of the inorganic world, and the biologic sciences for psychology, the ethnographical and social for moral and natural law, so various artistic criticism and the history of art and disciplines related thereto are a preparation for the philosophy of art.

Even if art criticism can ignore the philosophy of art (Michelangelo or Raphael never thought to discourse on the beautiful, and no one reproached them for not doing so), the philosophy of art cannot be separated from matters of artistic life. You may erect a building of one story, but if you build two stories, the second must necessarily rest upon the first. Philosophers who have remained strangers to the things of art have constructed only aesthetic theories which are artificial and a priori. Kant furnishes an example of this. He traveled little. He was "an aesthetic of the cell" who was never dragged away from his solitary meditations by visits to museums; he does not take account of aesthetic phenomena until a late hour, in the *Third Critique,* and only to give it a place as a rounding out of his whole philosophic system. Not that it is necessary, falling into the opposite excess, to require as preparations for the philosophical study of the beautiful, universal artistic initiation which even the professionals do not possess. Only exceptionally endowed natures—Plato, Plotinus, Schiller—join the temperament of artist and of art critic to that of a philosopher. There is a measure to be observed, and it is not impossible to determine it.

Method

From what has just been said one may conclude without difficulty that the philosophy of art ought to follow the inductive method: it ought to rise from observation to principles and laws. The times no longer tolerate the vague reveries of a Hegel or the vaporous speculations of a Victor Cousin, both of whom pretend to deduce from the notion of the Absolute Mind or from the concept of beauty a body of aesthetic formulas. From among the clouds the philosophy of art has returned to earth; it is anchored on the rock of reality.

Observation of artistic facts is the point of departure requisite for a study of beauty. This observation must be extended widely, not only including the works of the past, incomparable documents that mark off the course of centuries, but enriched by the living art of today, taking account of its evolutions. This observation should be not only of perfect productions where the nature of art shines out in its most intelligible forms but also of the artistic rudiments which one picks up among primitive peoples and prehistoric cultures. This observation is both internal and external, applying itself to works of art but not less to states of mind, because artistic productions are of the mind and therefore all psychological data, by psychophysiological method, find a place in the study of the philosophy of art.

Observation conducted strictly according to the demands of the inductive method will give rise to the ideas and laws which are interpretive of beauty and without which the present study would be deprived of its philosophic character. The philosophy of art, like every other philosophic science, should be pursued by the method which may be called analytico-synthetic.

DIVISIONS

The work of art is man's most accessible manifestation of beauty; it is the beautiful par excellence in the human order. It is in connection with the work of art that we shall set the general conditions of beauty, the notions of general aesthetics; secondarily, the beautiful in nature will be spoken of when the occasion arises to emphasize its relations with artistic beauty.

To classify the problems that will be brought into view in a philosophy of art, no better procedure can be found, it seems to us, than to adopt the plan drawn up by Aristotle, which responds to the most rigorous didactic demands. The master of intellectualism, this man with a passion for clear ideas and neat distinctions, remarks that in regard to all things one should put the triple question: from what does this thing come (that is, what is its origin); of what does it consist; what is its purpose?

Submissive to his counsel, we shall ask ourselves: (1) Who produces the work of art; what is its genesis? (chap. 2.) (2) In what does it consist; that is, what is its nature? (chaps. 3–7.) (3) What purpose does it serve: that is, what is its end or destination? (chap. 8.)

CHAPTER II

The Genesis of the Work of Art

G ENESIS, nature, mission (or finality): it is around these three headings that we will group the problems with which a philosophy of art is concerned, and we will give evidence, in proportion as we find the solution, to how fruitful and comprehensive these are.

Who produces the work of art, who is its "efficient cause"? It will not suffice to say, the artist. For at once the question will arise under a more precise form: what factors, what conditions control the artist in this production?

DOCUMENTARY SOURCES

Before answering, we should determine the documents whose study will furnish the solution. Now, to discover the origin of a work of art, to retrace the various phases implied in its elaboration, there are numerous records, some looming up from the past, the multiple unfoldings of the history of art or of those even farther removed into the prehistoric ages, others pertaining to living art, to productions unfolding before our very eyes. Cartoons, outlines, rough drafts, and first sketches, in which artists, fired with inspiration, embodied their original conceptions, all of these preparatory works have long been relegated to almost inaccessible corners of museums. This condition is unfortunate because they are incomparable psychological documents admirably revealing the history of a masterpiece.[1] To them must be added articles and autobiographies in which artists—Hector Berlioz, for one— have related numerous minor facts about the genesis of their works. Then we can also open the vast collection of what might be called elementary artistic data: careful psychologists such as Ricci, K. Gotze, Levinstein, and Rouma, have gathered, classified, and interpreted the drawings of children, simple beginnings in which we can observe the spontaneous awakening of the artistic sense.[2] Others have collected the aesthetic vestiges of prehistory, the efforts of primitive peoples still inhabiting various parts of the world, who resemble children in many ways. It does not matter how far back we go, even prehistoric man seems to have been engaged in sculpture and painting, in the adornment of his temples, homes, apparel, and tools. Like the most primitive of present-day primitives, he used geometric designs and decorative

[1] Their classification is taken from different angles. For example the *Handzel-zeichnungen Albertina* of Vienna.

[2] Levinstein, *Kinderzeichnungen* (Leipzig, 1905) collected 4,945 drawings by children; Conrad Ricci, *L'arte dei bambini,* 1887.

motifs, which are, it appears, the first forms in which the aesthetic sense manifests itself. The study of these important works of art enables us to grasp from their rough and unfinished state the activities and procedures whose full development creates perfect works. Rudimentary art throws light upon highly developed art, as the study of abnormal psychology enables us to understand that of the healthy and well-balanced. The same can be said, although true in a lesser degree, of the archaic works found in the beginnings of the various cycles comprising the history of art. Here then is a vast museum, the galleries of which are filled with documentary material, allowing us to follow step by step the multiform beginnings of artistic creation.

Classification of the Problems

Hence the doctrines explicative of the genesis of the work of art need not be invented out of whole cloth, but can be and ought to be based on abundant observation. Thus is verified what we have already remarked about the method of the philosophy of art: that it is anchored in the living rock of reality. In this connection many complex problems arise, which, it seems to us, can be divided into two groups: first, those in which the production of a work of art is regarded as an individual act; secondly, those in which it is seen as a social enterprise. The first group calls into service the principles of individual psychology; the second, those of social psychology.

The Work of Art an Entity

If we consider the creation of a work of art as an individual act, to every such work can be applied what Raphael said of his canvases: a person paints with his brain before he paints with his brush. The work exists in the head of the artist as a representation, an ideal, before it finds expression in the material elements in which his talent embodies it. Two moments may be noted in the production of an artistic work: the formation or conception of the ideal and its appearance in outward form, or its execution. Without the conception the work would be incoherent. Without the execution it would never evolve from the realm of ideas. It would live unknown in the world of the real, like many projects which artists, surprised by a premature death, carry with them to the grave. The work of art, then, is not the casual happy result of an instinctive activity, or the fruit of a vital urge, similar to that which incites the bee to fashion the honeycomb of wax or the beaver to construct his dam; otherwise how are we to explain the fact that great painters like Raphael, Leonardo da Vinci, and Memlinc tried many sketches, one correcting the other, which correspond to so many stages in the elaboration of the same subject?

We mean by "ideal" a mental representation which the man makes for himself of a work to be executed, of an end to be attained, before the actual execution of the work or the setting out to accomplish the end. The landscape gardener, the stone mason, or the runner has the notion in the large of what is to be accomplished: of the wall to be constructed, the stadium to be encircled; and this notion guides and sustains him.[3] It is not otherwise with the artistic ideal. Before putting his design on canvas or spreading his colors, Raphael conceived the images, alive and clear, of his "madonnas," with all the expression he was going to give them. Each image he worked over and over, trying to render it more and more the perfect reproduction of the model he carried within him, as is exemplified by the numerous pen sketches he made of his *Virgin of the Fields*.[4] The internal vision floated before his imagination, cherished and loved. Then it directed his hand and constituted the power which produced on the canvas. The artistic ideal is "clear intuition, a distinct image where the artist arranges the elements necessary to produce an impression of beauty."

A vaporous aesthetic of Platonic origin has existed, placing the ideal in an inaccessible region of absolute perfection. Superior by its definition to all that anyone can conceive, the ideal, for the holders of an exaggerated spiritualism after the manner of Victor Cousin, is nothing but an intangible and deceptive chimera. In this conception, the ideal of virtue would be vastly superior to the act of virtue which the literary man would be able to conceive or describe, and the most beau-

---

[3] The ideal is the exemplary cause which directs the action of the efficient cause endowed with intelligence. Before constructing a piece of furniture, writes St. Augustine, the carpenter must conceive the plan. "Faber facit arcam. Primo in arte habet arcam. Si enim in arte non haberet, non esset unde fabricando illam proferret. In arte invisibiliter est, in opere visibiliter erit." *Tract. I in Evang. Joan.*

[4] Preserved in the Albertina at Vienna.

tiful bodily form issuing from the chisel of Phidias would be only a shadow beside the ideal human body. Here is a confusion between the perfection in the sense of conformity to the demands of a type and the perfection which an artist seeks to realize in executing what he has conceived. The conception of a great artist has about it nothing of the fleeting or the undecided. With him vision, hearing, and touch are more sensitive and refined than with other men. Since his creative imagination is more fruitful, the inspirational image fixes itself in vivid outline; he sees and knows what he is going to produce before producing it; furthermore, he is not an artist at this price.

FORMATION OF THE IDEAL

How is the artistic ideal, thus understood, brought into being? Numerous factors contribute to its formation, some coming from without and others from the psychic powers of the artist.

The external factors are nature, race, and social environment. In the imitative arts the influence of the natural mold is evident. You will find in Murillo's Madonnas the Audalusian type, just as in the paintings of Ruysdael, the landscapes of Holland. The sunny countries are the countries of the vision; the misty regions, the veiled ones of the dream. In the stories of Daudet and the dramas of Ibsen you may discern respectively the sky of Provence or the atmosphere of Norway. The churches of the South where the light is garish and abundant have comparatively small openings for light and these are adequate; whereas the Gothic cathedrals of the northern countries spread wide their many and large windows to capture all the light possible.

Race plays a role not less important. Do not certain peoples, such as the ancient Greeks, seem to have been privileged by nature, and others seem to have been well-nigh disinherited? The influence of race is often combined with that of social environment which, over and above the racial, makes its contribution, and causes to arise a much discussed problem: precisely what is the influence of the social environment upon a given artist; more specifically, what is the influence of his artistic environment?

You cannot miss it. The artistic environment is the atmosphere which the artist breathes and with which he is impregnated. Three-fourths of the artists owe their technique to the school of a master who trains them and decides the direction of their talent. Even those who blaze new trails, a Leonardo da Vinci, a Rubens, a J. S. Bach, are not able to escape the influence of their predecessors. Leonardo follows Verrochio, Rubens studies the Italians and bears the imprint of Quentin Metseys; Sebastian Bach finds his precedents in the school of his uncle. Moments come when the genius of a whole artistic period becomes crystallized and places in honor "a small number of characteristic procedures, by means of which artists realize the unity of the work of art." It is the style. In the matter of furniture, for instance, there is the style of Louis XV, of Louis XVI; in architecture, the Roman style or the Gothic. The taste of contemporaries decides the longevity of a style, but the artist is influenced by the same taste and often accommodates himself to it; for there is required a powerful and audacious nature to fly in the face of contemporary demand and to turn one's art into new channels.

Physical environment, race, social climate: these three factors would be sufficient, following an artistic determinism, to explain the production of a work of art, just as they explain the appearance of the artist himself. Taine has contrived to show that artists are human plants growing in a society like grain in a fertile soil. If he can write of intelligence that it is a product "similar to sugar or sulphuric acid," we understand what he means when he says of Holland: "In this country water makes the grass, which produces the cattle, which makes the cheese, the butter, and the meat, and which all together result in the native inhabitant." [5] They make him flabby of cast and slow of step, and they produce also the Holland artist and his art, products of greater complexity, no doubt, but not less markedly the output of the environment. Almost magical talent was required to mask the insufficiencies of this theory of environment put forth by Taine and given such excessive and fatalistic significance. Sow the grain with a lavish hand in a soil prepared for it, and the frail stalks of the nourished plant will rise thousandfold. Why, then, if the artistic plant is of such a nature, has there been only one Rubens in the Antwerpian metropolis of the seventeenth century, a soil so well prepared for the outflowering of talent?

[5] Taine, *Philosophie de l'art* (2nd ed., 1872), p. 55.

Why did not Rubenses arise in myriads? Why did the greater
number of those who frequented his school produce nothing
but mediocre paintings, mere studio studies? Why did not
Van Dyck, whom he drew to follow in his footsteps and fashioned with jealous care in his own image, hesitate to be his
real self and to commit to canvas the personal inspirations of
his own rich temperament? Why was Raphael not Michelangelo, and why, of the two Corneille brothers, both reared
in the same environment, did one become a great poet and the
other a simple versifier?

It is because neither the models of nature nor their influence of race nor the traditions of a school nor the fashion of
an epoch nor the artistic climate accounts fully for the formation of works of art, or the ideal which inspires them. An
artistic production is marked with the imprint of a personality, and for this reason it has the right to be called a creation.
Full of enthusiasm in contemplation of the nobility of artistic
activity, Dante Alighieri compares it to that of almighty God
Himself:

> . . . *che vostra arte a Deo quasi nepote.*
>
> Inferno, XI, 103

Art is the grandson of God, for it is begotten of the creative
power of man, as man himself issues from the hands of God.
What is most elevating and ravishing in art man draws from
his own being. And when that man is named Homer or
Phidias, Dante or Giotto, Michelangelo or Raphael, Beethoven or Wagner, personality asserts itself so imperiously that

the work, teeming with riches of the artist's nature, commands the environment after having obeyed it and blazes a new trail.

The internal factors of the artistic production, the creative powers of the artist, are the external senses, the imagination, and the intellect; and in every work of art their action is evident. Certainly there is need for a special technique and mode as regards statues or monuments, paintings or symphonies; but the creative imagination and the intellect are what give a sense, a voice to stones and colors, to sounds and words. We shall point out farther on, in a discussion of the nature of the accomplished work embodying the ideal, what part belongs to one and to the other of the aesthetic faculties. The analysis of definite works left by the great artist indicates the process by which the ideal came into being.

THE IDEAL IN RUDIMENTARY ART

But already the intervention of the imagination and the intellect is revealed in the preliminary activities of the great masters, the progressive transformations of which permit us to follow the dynamic power of an idea. Furthermore, in the naive productions of children and primitives, we may recognize the rough indication of the creative urge, the crude contribution of a personality. The designs of children collected from the schools dominated by Western culture, or from the tents of Eskimos, or the huts of the Australian archipelago; figures chiseled in stone or traced on the walls of caves by men of the stone age (and one may add the works of archaic periods), attest that the objects are not executed as they appear to be but as they are imagined or conceived. This statement is worth some thought. Its value is evident in at least three particulars.

First is the process of schematization. Children and primitives conventionalize their objects; they put in their drawings only what appears essential to them; and their point of view, as we may readily see, is extremely variable. In a way, a head, a trunk, and two legs sum up the human body. In proportion as the young artist grows in age, the work is completed by the insertion of the neck, the hair, the beard, and the eyebrows. The child who regards the use of tobacco as a sign of superiority, places a pipe in the mouth of his personages; the Bakairi forget to mark the mouth, but they emphasize the nose, which they are accustomed to perforate; and the Bororos, whose custom it is to slit the lower lip, are careful to insert the mouth, but sometimes forget the nose.[6]

Secondly, all these designers treat separately each part of the object drawn without regard to the demands of proportion to the whole; it is not uncommon to see on a small body, hands too large, poorly drawn, and furnished with enormous rings.

Lastly, and most significantly, logic makes up for the insufficiencies of the design. Under a hat can be seen the hair; under the coat, the outline of the body; the stomach is visible in a clothed body; a profile is furnished with two eyes staring you in the face; and on the other hand, a front view of the

[6] Van der Steinen, *Unter den Naturvölkern* (Leipzig, 1894), p. 253.

face possesses a prominent nose drawn on the side and this sometimes serves the double purpose of a second visible one. They show what is inside houses or boats; Eskimo children draw a tent and in it the scenes representing the life passed there.[7] The stone-age man draws the heart of the elephant he sketches.[8] Is this not a proof that the child and the primitive man are not simple imitators but logicians? Impressed by a detail they consider characteristic, they search for all the means possible to put it in relief. Their imagination and intellect have made the plan of the finished drawing.

Several of these particularities, notably the mixture of profile and front view of the face, the design showing the outline of the body under draperies, are found in a large number of Egyptian subjects. In like manner the archaic epoch of Greek art offers examples of logical schematization, where, contrary to perspective and verity, is represented, over and above what one sees, that which one wishes to see but cannot. Dorian ceramic vases present funeral scenes showing the procession in profile while certain portions of the corpse are so arranged fronting the spectator that all its parts may be recognized.

We find these same features in the early painting of the Flemish and Italian schools. The great masters themselves sometimes revert to the bilocal procedure, which is a vestige of the archaic. The *Life of Saint Bavo* by Rubens sums up on the same canvas two fundamental scenes from the life of the

[7] Levinstein, *op. cit.,* figs. 75, 14, 106, etc.
[8] Henry Fairfield Osborn, *Men of the Old Stone Age* (New York, 1915), p. 316.

saint. Memlinc arranges in compartments of one picture all the episodes of the passion of Christ.

During the infancy of art, as during its maturity, man adds himself to nature, to the race, and to the environment: *Homo additus naturae*. Even before externalizing, the artist marks his conception with the seal of his personality.

The representative aspect, the intellectualist, of the ideal or of the artistic conception which we are now considering constitutes the fundamental element but not the only one. For the representation arouses loves and enthusiasms, stirs up the emotions and profound sentiments, since the artist is the first to enjoy his work while it is still imprisoned within its psychic envelope. He enjoys it in anticipation. In order not to expose ourselves to useless repetition, we shall study later the emotional character of art (chap. 6).

Externalizing the Ideal

But soon the idea which the artist bears within him acquires a dynamic power, it becomes a force, and sooner or later it engenders what Cherbuliez calls "this fatal penchant that pushes us in spite of ourselves to give a form to what we have in our heads, to show to others what we have seen, to make them feel what we have felt." [9] The work then enters the second phase, and the ideal is expressed externally.

The interior melody sings in the musician's ears, and he fixes it in his notations; the vision pursues the poet, and he reclothes it in a literary dress; the image floats before the

[9] Cherbuliez, *L'art et la nature*, Part III, chap. 13.

painter, the sculptor, the architect, rich in colors, fair in form, and he does his best to work it into materials manipulated by his skillful hands.

The need, not simply to imitate nature, but to interpret and dominate reality, the joy of giving to stones, to sounds, to colors a meaning at once personal and universal, the feeling of mastering the material and of subjecting it to an idea into which a person has put the best of himself explain sufficiently, it seems, the externalization of the ideal in a material medium. We cannot look for the origin of the work in the automatic overflow of the active impulse, in the expenditure of energies not needed for maintaining the individual's life. When the kitten is fed up, says Herbert Spencer, he plays with a ball of yarn in order to utilize his superfluous muscular energy, quite as a giraffe in the zoo gnaws at the barriers of his cage. Thus it is supposed to be with human beings; the herdsman who sings to avoid leaving his throat to a spiritless inactivity, the child who, seated at table, becomes impatient for his dinner and makes the semblance of eating from an empty plate, would be yielding to the aesthetic urge. Aesthetic activity is the use of an energy which has not a useful purpose, and which a person exercises for the sake of exercising it. The work of art is born when, all needs being satisfied, a reserve of energy remains expendable. In the measure in which scientific progress economizes the human forces necessary to physical well-being and to comfort, these reserves of energy which man may put at the service of art will increase.

Thus art is aimless play and an activity of luxury. These two formulas were invented by Kant and taken over, though in a different sense, by Herbert Spencer to great advantage. They explain well enough, and this we will speak of later, the aspect of disinterestedness of the artistic emotion, but not the genesis of art. The positivist theory of play deprives art of its seriousness and its dignity; it reduces it to comic antics; it places on the same footing sport and art, football and music or painting; it makes no distinction between the sportive leaps of a cat and the efforts of a great artist. It either mistakes these latter or does them violence. How many men, in fact, favored with health and fortune, devote to things altogether different from art those reserves of energy they have to dispose of! On the other hand, how many great artists, grappling with the difficulties of life, have, in spite of every obstacle, obeyed their inspiration, have braved poverty and social injustice to follow the interior voice that lured them on! The history of art has also its martyrology, filled with manifestations of heroism similar to those of martyrs for the faith.

Some have tried to attribute paleolithic works of art to a utilitarian preoccupation: the primitives obeyed the idea that the representation of the reindeer on the walls of the cavern served to attract the animal or facilitate its capture, so that, in the words of Reinach, the art of primitives was "magic." But it has been justly remarked that the representations of animals are explained equally as well by attributing them to a disinterested motive, and that the drawings of numerous and varied human figures does not accommodate itself at all to the utilitarian explanation.[10] The designs of the primitives are as crude as their conceptions, but they satisfy the psychological need of outward expression.

If you ask what relations exist between the two phases of the artistic ideal, between its mental formation and its execution, it can be said that the second is always logically dependent on the first and is oftenest chronologically posterior to it. Some keep the image within them a long time before they give it material expression, others execute step by step as they go along, and others begin by executing the ideal in its entirety, which enriches and perfects itself in the very process of its execution. It is with the artistic ideal as with the "directive idea" in the sciences which Claude Bernard speaks of: now it springs forth in a flash, at a moment when least expected; at another time it must be sought after, resists desire, and shines out brightly only after long effort. "I improvised the *March of the Pilgrims* in two hours while in revery before the fireplace," writes Hector Berlioz in his memoirs, "and in the course of six years I introduced modifications that have, I believe, improved it." [11] Others, on the contrary, like Rubens, meditated little and abandoned themselves to the resources of their nature; for them it was not far from the idea to the canvas. Nevertheless the fire of enthusiasm did not exclude the clear vision of the end to be attained.

The outward execution of the artistic conception demands

[10] Luquet. "Le problème des origines de l'art et l'art paléolithique," *Revue philosophique,* May, 1913.
[11] H. H. Berlioz, *Mémoires* (ed. Calman Levy), I, 303.

technical skill which nothing else can supply: every artist possesses high sensitivity; he is a specialist in some manner, in what he sees or hears in color or design. Moreover, whatever may be the result of his effort, it never responds adequately to the conception; and this it is that explains how rarely artists are satisfied with their work. If Michelangelo, as is said, fell in love with his Moses, how many others have been obliged to destroy remarkably good works! For the ideal realized is never the ideal conceived. "Look me in the eye," remarks Cherbuliez, "and there you will see the world; look at my works, and you will find there only what I have been able to say; and I swear to you that what I have not said is the more beautiful. My feelings are a stream from which I have been condemned to dip with watering pot quite too small. In vain do I remove its stopper to discharge the water through its neck; the water that comes out of it is only a drop compared with what flows in the river. You have told me just now that my picture is going to be wonderful. Go on; do not restrain yourself; treat it like a masterpiece; I shall never finish it. When I compare it to the other, to that which is in my soul, in my nerves, in my eyes, I know only too well all it lacks." More than any other person the artist realizes his defects. Is this not a new proof of the clearness of the internal image which the work of art but imperfectly copies?

The Work of Art as a Social Factor

Regarded as a social fact, art is involved with the vast network of psychic elements which form a civilization; and we

do not dream of discussing the many complex questions which, from this new point of view, are related to its genesis and scope.

Let us limit ourselves to pointing out this one fact, that complete artistic development is intimately connected with high economic achievement, autonomy, and political freedom: art, like science and philosophy, is the daughter of progress and liberty. The Memphis of the Pyramid builders, the Thebes of Rameses II, the Athens of Pericles, the Byzantium of Justinian, the Ravenna of the fifth century, the Rome of the popes, the Florence of the Medici at the time of the Renaissance, and the Paris of Louis XIV, all escaped the depressing action of war and were environments suitable for the flourishing of art; art, though a delicate plant, pushes its way up of its own accord in cultures sufficiently rich.

For the same reason art loves capitals; it avails itself fully of the luxury which they enjoy and it flourishes there by the favor of the powerful. When the axis of the Greek world shifted, art migrated from Athens to Alexandria, as later it found its way to Rome. Our modern metropolises, like those of former time, are artistic centers; they afford artists consecration and fame.

Let us enunciate still another law by saying that this flower of culture, art, yields to the influence of other social factors. It is a soft wax that receives the imprint of religion, of science, and of philosophy. Nothing manifests more clearly the interaction of these elements as they cross and penetrate into one another.

In the first place stands religion, which is one of the chief inspirers of art. Notice the role that divinity plays in the monuments of the Egyptians, the place of Greek mythology in ancient sculpture, and especially the imprint of Christianity on the art of the Middle Ages and of the Renaissance. The cathedrals were works of beauty and also sanctuaries of prayer; history contained in the Old and the New Testament furnished the principal themes of stained glass, painting, and sculpture throughout the Middle Ages; and if you should remove religious subjects from the Italian art of the Renaissance, the museums of Florence or of Rome would retain little of their greatness.

In a lesser degree but real, the art of an era bears the seal of the dominant preoccupation of learning. Let us cite here merely the numerous representations of the liberal arts which the Middle Ages have left in their miniatures, their stained glass, their cloisters; the canvases of Traini (at Pisa), of Gozzoli (at the Louvre), which symbolize the heated discussions carried on by philosophers in the thirteenth century; or again, the scientific allegories of Raphael or of Michelangelo.[12]

Inversely art spreads like a beneficent dew over the whole field of social life and is affected by the moral atmosphere. Of this latter we shall speak farther on.

[12] See our work *Civilization and Philosophy in the Middle Ages* (Princeton University Press, 1920), chap. 7. This work contains the Vanuxem Lectures which I gave at the University of Princeton in April, 1920.

CHAPTER III

The Nature of Works of Art

THE present chapter and the following ones bring us to the heart of the fundamental problem: What is the nature of works of art?

To this question the first answer, the simplest and seemingly the best, is this: a work of art is a thing expressive of beauty. It is as closely bound up with beauty as is a ruddy complexion with youth or the blooming of roses with summer. Common sense rejects the idea of a divorce between art and beauty. Yet the first philosopher who undertook to establish a theory of art, Plato, teaches that art has nothing in common with the beautiful. Through a strange anomaly this penetrating thinker, who was likewise an artist, whose dialogues are replete with poetry, and who as an accomplished Athenian practiced in his youth the arts of music and dancing, finds no words to apply to art except those of disdain. The deep reason for this attitude lies in his failure to understand the true nature of art. Art for Plato is nothing but the imitation of the natural object, and the natural object itself is but a pale reflection of the real, which maintains an existence above sensible things and outside of them, in such a way that the work of art is twice removed from reality: a shadow of a shadow. The conclusion then follows that, compared with the original, the copy has little value. Placed beside the real, it is but wan and poor. Periodically along the route of history these strange disparagements of art are repeated. Leibnitz the optimist, Pascal the mystic, Diderot the materialist, all seek to disparage the work of man in order to exalt the more the work of nature. But these voices remain isolated, discordant, and are smothered by the voice of humanity which has loudly declared for twenty-three centuries: "The value of a work of art does not come from resemblance to a model but from itself. It has its own beauty." This has never been doubted less than today when the work of art is placed so high in the scale of values that some even worship it with a cult. Certain mystics and fanatics, such as Tolstoi, have recently repeated some of Plato's denunciations and have asserted that art is in no way defined by beauty; [1] but we must consider their remarks as paradoxical and mere whimsy.

How much more attractive and encouraging is the medieval notion that not only does every work of art manifest beauty, but the capability of doing so belongs to every product of human handicraft.

[1] "To appreciate a work of art according to its beauty, is as strange as to judge of the fertility of the soil by the beauty of the site." Tolstoi, *Qu'est-ce que l'art* (3rd ed.), p. 187.

The Beautiful Thing

We then assume provisionally that which will be readily seen throughout what follows, that the artistic work is expressive of beauty. Indeed more, it is the beautiful par excellence on the human level. This means that artistic beauty is more accessible to us than the beauty of nature; and, understanding it better, we like it more. To grasp the beauty of a landscape, a panorama, a stretch of sea or an Alpine view, we need the faculty of concentration and of contemplation, a degree of intellectual development not possessed by a large number. The man of the fields who lives close to nature rarely comes to enjoy its beauty, and many an urbanite views its marvels without comprehending them. The fact is that nature reveals her beauty to an elite few, and we shall say further that many even of those who believe they comprehend her beauty really enjoy only her benefactions.

The work of art, on the contrary, is made to speak to our souls; in popular art or aristocratic art, art of the museum or of the drawing room, its language of beauty is appropriate to all degrees of human nature. The reason for this fact seems to me to reside in the imprint of personality with which the artist marks his work, an imprint which renders it more intelligible and more resplendent than that of nature. Herein lies the secret of the universal prestige which works of art have ever enjoyed, and will enjoy in all societies where good sense has not been discarded. "I am a man, and nothing human is alien to me." This verse of Terence can be applied in the fullest sense to artistic creation.

From this consideration a corollary results which evokes a question of method. If the highest beauty known to man lies in a work of art and not in nature, it is as a function of the former that we should study the latter, and the constitutive theories of general aesthetics should be based primarily on artistic reality. In this sense we can say with Bergson: "It seems more comfortable to the rules of a sane method to study beauty first in works where it has been produced by a conscious effort and to pass thence through imperceptible transitions to nature, an artist in her own way." [2]

SUBJECTIVE AND OBJECTIVE ASPECTS

So far we have done nothing more than define the status of the question and establish certain prolegomena. It is understood that art is expressive of beauty, and beauty on the human level. But what is artistic beauty? Immediately two contradictory answers present themselves, philosophical antinomies: is beauty in the work itself; or is it confined to the impressions that fill our souls? Is it a property of things or an internal elaboration of our own? Is it outside us, or within us? The Greeks concentrated their attention on the objective aspects of beauty: order, symmetry, or even the profundity of being. But modern and contemporary philosophy turn us toward the other pole of thought; it sees in artistic beauty only subjective elements and it studies them with all the resources of psychological analysis. The theory is current today that beauty belongs in no way to the work of art. Benedetto Croce, who passes for an intellectual in Italy, be-

[2] H. Bergson, *Données immédiates de la conscience*, p. 11.

gins a recent treatise on aesthetics with this declaration: "Beauty does not inhere in things; it is not a physical fact; it belongs to man's activity, to spiritual energy." [3] Lipps speaks the same language, and we might easily multiply citations.[4] Here we have artistic subjectivism.

I hope to show that the truth lies between the two extremes; that the Greek point of view, instead of being incompatible with the modern, helps to fructify and integrate the latter; and the artistic beauty implies both technical and objective elements on the part of the work, and impression on the part of the observer; so that beauty is the result born of an intimate correlation of the two.

Thus the beauty of a work of art is complex, bilateral, since it resides at one and the same time in the object marked with its imprint and in the subject who contemplates it. The two aspects which it presents are inseparable. They are not juxtaposed but penetrate each other. When we speak of the role of the object, we must always keep in mind that of the subject, and vice versa. Only for didactic reasons do we dissociate the two aspects and treat the objective factors of a work of art separately from the subjective impression which it produces. This final remark serves to justify the plan we shall follow in this work.

[3] Croce, *Esthétique comme science de l'expression et linguistique générale* (French tr., Paris, 1904), p. 93.

[4] "The beauty of an object is not a property of that object, as green and blue." Lipps, "Aesthetik" in *Die Cultur der Gegenwart*, VI (1907), 93.

CHAPTER IV

The Artistic Order

THE IDEA OF ORDER

A PERSON wishes to set his library in order. Will he pile up haphazardly books and reviews, newspapers and essays, brochures and manuscripts as does the truckman when he loads his wagon with them? That would not be order, but chaos. On the contrary, will he not rather make a careful classification, arranging each group on its designated shelf: for example, the novels here, the travelogues there, the works of philosophy by themselves, scientific treatises, studies of art, histories, and so on, each group in its respective place? This simple illustration will enable us to understand what order is and what it implies.

First of all we know that order never exists without a plurality of elements. The simple has no need of being placed in order.[1] The thought will never occur to a man to systematize his library if he has only one book. Even a person who has but two books, were he to be concerned about their orderly arrangement, would be the object of ridicule. Two books can no more make a library than two sunshiny days a summer. How many books are required? I do not know, and it does not matter. What is important is that there must be a plurality, and this plurality of elements forms the material from which order will radiate, the substratum which will be the foundation of its existence. How will this existence, this radiation, be assured? By reduction to unity according to the principle of classification.

Unity is the second element of order.[2] When I arrange my library, as in the aforementioned example, and put on special shelves the books, brochures, reviews, and newspapers which pertain to particular subjects, I arrange them according to their contents: the principle of classification here is ideological. I can choose other bases of unity; for one example, the language in which the different works are written, and immediately the order in my library changes its aspect: works on law, on science, on philosophy are grouped together according as they are in Latin, French, or English. I can consider other principles of unification. Thus I may arrange my books according to size or the color of their binding. Some persons

---

[1] "Ordo in ratione sua includit tria, scilicet: . . . distinctionem, quia non est ordo aliquorum nisi distinctorum." St. Thomas, *Comm. in Lib. I Sentent.*, dist. XX, q. 1, a. 3.

[2] "Includit etiam tertio rationem ordinis, ex qua etiam ordo in speciem contrahitur. Unde unus est ordo secundum locum, alius secundum dignitatem, alius secundum originem et sic de aliis." *Ibid.*

have recourse to this superficial system, for in their case the library must afford pleasure to the eye. The keepers of large deposits of books hold to a numerical classification based on the class designation which the work received on its entry, and this principle of unity answers admirably to the needs of the public libraries.

All these examples place in relief the essence of the principle of unity: "it is a design of the mind, a content of ideas, detached from matter and, we do not hesitate to add, detached by way of abstraction from the whole mass of material in the working out of a pattern." Following the forthright formula of a philosopher of the Middle Ages, we may say that unity is the rational element of order: *ratio ordinis*.

The term "abstraction" need not frighten us. The element of reality which we take hold of by the process of abstraction is not necessarily, as some think, a metaphysical and suprasensible thing, such as virtue or goodness. Quite the contrary; abstraction is rooted primarily in the domain of sensibility. The arrangement of height in a regiment, which from left to right, from right to left, places the soldiers according to an ascending or a descending scale, rests on the principle of unity recognized by the senses: the size of the body. The same holds true in different arts: the Roman or Gothic arch, the magnificent repetitions of which produced the naves of the churches and the cathedrals of France, are linear forms seen with the eyes but perceived in an abstract way as the principle of unity.

From this idea of the principle of unity arise a number of consequences of which we shall have to make numerous applications in the study of the work of art. On the other hand, the number of materials set in order does not influence the nature of the order; the ideological principle, for example, shown by a number inscribed on the back of a book, applies in the same manner in a small library of a private person as in immense public collections where the books are gathered by hundreds of thousands. On the other hand, the element of specification may be the principle of unity. Thus order is determined by it. Change the principle of unity, and the arrangement of materials is modified immediately. Furthermore, the order of one may become the disorder of the other. A lawyer or a professor will find his desk in order when the documents, the books, the pamphlets are placed in ideological groups according to the functions of the works he uses in his profession: for the valet, on the contrary, this arrangement of materials is meaningless, and all those who are accustomed to having loaded study desks know that only the strictest commands can prevent servants from arranging the contents according to the size of the books, the shape of the pamphlets, and the dimensional appearances of the papers. If one would call the valet's attention to the fact that he has here put the papers in disorder, the latter is surprised. Why? Because he did not understand, he did not perceive the principle of order which inspired his master's arrangement; his mind failed to grasp the situation from the point of view of unity: in our example, the ideological contents of the documents concerned. He resembles in this case the peasant of Dauphine who is wholly insensible to the marvelous order of the mountains or of the environment where he lives; or he is like the uncultured visitor who, placed before the *Victory of Samothrace* at the turn of the great stairs in the Louvre, does not complete in his imagination the mutilated members of this winged woman and does not perceive the impression of grace, of pride, and of power that this marble was to give on the prow of the ship.

Let us remark again that when any one order is made by man, man chooses freely his principle of unity; but once he has chosen it he must remain faithful to it under the risk of diminishing the force and enterprise of the idea which unifies. The organizers of our great libraries know it well: a misplaced book is nearly always a lost book. The intellect finds unity a necessity, yearns for it, and takes delight in it. From instinct man's mind classifies and groups things around one center, and this is so imperative that where a real unity is lacking, the mind establishes an artificial unity in things. Inversely, disorder hampers us and makes us suffer. When this is evident, as happens in a defective work of art, it is outrightly painful to the soul.

Multiplicity of materials and the principle of unity are the two elements we have considered up to now. There is a third, variety, which is to say that the arranged elements ought to carry within them in different degrees the common characters that the intellect chooses as a principle of order.[3] All the books of the library scientifically arranged do not treat of the

[3] "Rationem prioris et posterioris; unde secundum omnes illos modos potest dici esse ordo aliquorum, secundum quos aliquis altero prius dicitur et secundum locum et secundum tempus et secundum omnia huiusmodi." *Ibid.*

same subject; and even in the same branch of knowledge, as in law, for example, we know that the works which have been published on legal questions do not all possess the same value nor do they all have the same importance.

But varied does not mean disparate. Variety supposes common elements; disparity excludes all common ground and renders impossible a reduction to unity or any participation in the principle of order. There is a disparity between men and numerical figures, between scientific judgments and giraffes. How do you hope to place in the same order of entities such things as do not possess anything of that similarity which only the mind can grasp, having abstracted it from the designated materials? Rather we class men with men, ideas with ideas. If, for example, we arrange the soldiers in a regiment according to their height, we perceive that their height varies: the relation existing between the heights of any two of them and the standard of measure is not the same. Thus it is with the order in a watch, in a locomotive, where all the materials (here it is a matter of machinery) have not the same importance, but contribute, while fulfilling distinct functions, to the production of the same movement (the movement of the hands on a dial, of the wheels on the rails), and this movement is the principle of unity of the watch or of the locomotive. It is the same in the chronological order, the social, and the military: we could indefinitely prolong this list of examples. Order, then, may be defined as "the reduction to unity of multiple and varied elements according to the same principle or common plan."

Types of Order

This elementary idea of order enables us to put into one class the different types which the order presupposes. The field of order is as vast as that of being. All the real and all the conceivable are susceptible of being arranged mentally in various homogeneous groups. Running over existing things in the mind in view of the basis of classification, we can establish multiple divisions of order. The following are the two principal ones.

When a person systematizes the contents of knowledge (ideas and judgment), the order is logical or scientific; when he classifies real beings, things existing outside himself, the order is real. It is with judgments and reasons as materials that one constructs a science (logical order), as it is with bricks and lumber that we use for building houses (real order).

Real order can be classed as static or dynamic, an order of coordination or of subordination. The mechanical order (locomotive, automobile, watch) is based on function (rapid movement, indication of time); the social order rests on the multiplication of relationships in the various activities which citizens carry on; the order of a bank or railroad station depends on some determined objective (security and rapidity of the operations of financiers, movement of trains and of travelers). Examples of the dynamic order are to be found where the dominating principle is the destination desired, the activity to be accomplished, the end to be pursued.

On the other hand, the static order does not awaken any idea of a final purpose; one thing is realized or unfolded by the simple setting of its elements in full view; e.g., the order of the groups in a procession, the disposition of a clump of trees, and the steps in the hierarchy of honors, as in the Legion of Honor, are static orders.

The two orders, static and dynamic, may appear in the same being. A race horse and a draught-horse, in repose, show the same coordination of muscles, the some configuration of the body which characterizes any horse as a horse (static order). But let them move ever so little, and immediately the movement of the muscles and of the limbs is directed toward a special and different end for each, rapidity of movement in one case, slow drawing of a heavy load in the other (dynamic form).

Nature in her production, too, directs the constitution of a thing toward its end. The cattle-breeder, for instance, although bending nature to his design, must still bow to the great law of finality.

One will see that the artistic order is an order of things and not an order of ideas; and this real order is at the same time static and dynamic. To understand it we must pass from the general idea of order to the idea of artistic order and take account of what the second adds to the first.

Artistic Order

Is any kind of order that man may achieve in material objects (in colors, in sounds, in shapes) the order of artistic beauty? No, assuredly not. A library, a shop-window of magazines, a well-kept grocery store, a book of measurements, or a mechanic's box of tools may be well ordered without being marked at all with the artistic seal. When then, according to the aforementioned conditions, does an ordered work become covered with the royal mantle of beauty? We will answer: "When it is capable of producing a powerful impression on the subject which it contacts, when it will speak plainly and clearly to his senses, to his imagination, to his intellect; when all its elements will call out and stimulate this pleasure of contemplation which constitutes the primary artistic end." More briefly, the artistic order is an order powerfully expressed and brilliant in its clarity. A work of art is a completely ordered thing; which means that it contains a multiplicity of elements, that it is made up of variety, that it has unity. But the order is powerfully expressed; that is to say, the artist applies himself continually to the adaptation of the realized order to the work of lively contemplation which he must awaken. The more perfect this adaptation, the more does the work achieve beauty. All artistic efforts aim to facilitate this work of contemplation. Thus the artistic order is not an absolute thing since it must adapt itself to the capacities of the subject.

These are formulas, you may say. Yes, but vivifying formulas, for they explain by this law of correlation the artistic exigencies, the procedures of art. Let us examine a few of those procedures, grouping them around constitutive elements of the artistic order.

Artistic Multiplicity

Let us speak, first of all, of the multiplicity of elements that enter into a work of art: of what Aristotle calls the desired grandeur or just measure,[4] integrity, and magnitude. We can easily see that this multiplicity is a function of the impression to be produced on the spectator or auditor and hence it has the possibility of being too poor or too rich.

If too poor in elements, the work will be paltry, banal, unable to interest: a black point on a white board does not answer to the demand of artistic execution; a reflection in the manner of Bernard Pallissy is not of literary value. Let us note, however, that what appears insignificant in itself, may, in the hands of an artist, become redolent of beauty. A procession coming out of church, a ray of sunlight on the thatch of a hut, an evening indoor scene, and a thousand other subjects furnish matters of complex relations to the painter, to the designer or water-colorist, who knows how to put them into artistic presentation.[5]

If, on the contrary, the work of art accumulates so many details that the observer cannot encompass everything in one look, the pleasure of the artistic contemplation is spoiled at its source, and the work sins by excess against the above-

---

[4] *Poetica,* VII, 4.

[5] It is the same with natural beauty: the movement of a swimmer who plunges into the water is well ordered if he has an equation between the effort spent and the end attained (ontological order): and this order has nothing aesthetic about it. If, however, we learn that a thought of heroic courage inspires him, if it is a question of a perilous rescuing, the act of throwing oneself into the water, banal in itself, may borrow under the circumstances, a tragic beauty.

mentioned law of correlation. Complexity then becomes a hindrance. This is the impression which is left at the Museum of Versailles by the immense paintings of battles that cover the walls of the long galleries. They are for the most part strategic panoramas with incoherent episodes intermingled, and neither the mind nor the eye is able to coordinate them. Perhaps there reigns in these pictures a strategic order (ontological order), but the artistic value is compromised by the difficulty or impossibility which a beholder experiences in attempting to perceive it in its entirety (artistic order). This is the impression which certain modern musical compositions produce in their misuse of the resources of the orchestra.

But there is a whole series of artistic procedures the analysis of which will show that the multiplicity of the constitutive elements of a work of art must not be viewed in an absolute way as natural beauty, but in a relative way, according to the capacity of the subject called upon to contemplate it. A missioner relates that a Negro to whom he showed the photograph of a horseman in profile turned the picture on all sides to discover the second leg on the other side of the horse. A little incident like this shows the difference between the whole naturally ordered and the whole artistically ordered. In nature a being is in order and will be beautiful only if it possesses in reality the integral parts which its perfection requires, and on this account a man with an integral part of his body missing or impaired in one of its functions is deprived of natural beauty and that in the measure to which he is mutilated. "A small man, no matter how well-proportioned in his littleness, will never be beautiful for he lacks the proper height; he must compensate for it by being all the more gentle and courteous." [6] In the artistic order the case is otherwise; it suffices that the order appears, and makes the impression of a complete being. The actual presence of all the elements is not a requisite. This completeness is so little needed that the artist may devote himself freely to the mutilations proper to the nature of the work, for he knows that to interest the spectator or auditor he must arouse in the latter creative activity; it is necessary to oblige him to fill in by his senses, by his imagination, by his intellect, the gaps established intentionally in the work, and to this effect certain elements being suggested draw others in their wake.

The procedures of mutilation and of artistic suggestion are practiced in all arts. In novels, tragedies, comedies, dramas, in a simple literary description, their use is a prime requisite. A novel which would display in minute detail and without taking anything for granted, the least actions and words of the characters would be insupportable. From one chapter to another the good writer presents certain things and he passes in silence intermediary facts, but the work contains the elements necessary for setting in action the imagination of the reader for the reconstruction of the whole plot. Through the silences practiced by his characters John Galsworthy produces striking effects in his novels. Racine makes us understand the im-

[6] "Dicit (Philosophus) quod pulchritudo non est nisi in magno corpore. Unde parvi homines possunt dici commensurati et formosi, sed non pulchri." St. Thomas, *op. cit.,* dist. XXXI, q.2, a.1.

portance of an event by showing its effect on an actor of the drama. That is what is called a duplication of the effect. The duplication of effect may even exist in the second degree. They are the words of Mr. Lachalas, and he makes us see that the procedure is applied too minutely, moreover, in a drama of Maeterlinck.[7] When Ernest Hello requires of the style that it be at the same time expansive and continuous, but that it have reserve and discretion, he refers to this act of abridgment which cannot be taught but which we recognize in the masters. The great poet, the great novelist, the great litterateur is the one who knows how to refrain from outward expression and how to transform his readers into poets, novelists, and litterateurs. It cannot be otherwise with the successful orator whose hinted implications exercise no less influence on the audience than the expressed discourse itself. In painting, an imaginative suggestion can add the element of depth to the representation. "Here the designer traces the arm of a woman; how is he to indicate that this arm is not flat but round, that it has relief? If there were only a bracelet at the wrist: I design this bracelet, and immediately the whole arm appears round. The form of the bracelet at the wrist indicated clearly, by the perspective, the rounded shape of the arm; the suggestion by which it operated at one point causes it to extend to the entire figure." [8]

[7] Lechalas, *Etudes esthétiques,* p. 135.
[8] Souriau, *La suggestion dans l'art,* p. 95. Cf. Lechalas. *Etudes esthétiques,* Paris, 1902, chap. 4. The suggestion which we have just spoken of is individual; it brightens the work from the interior since it contributes to make it enjoyable. Is there need of saying that it has nothing in common with collective suggestion or command, phenomena of the social order, but not of the aesthetic,

It is the same in music. Once the melody has been set, often the musician satisfies himself with evoking it in the course of the composition by a fragment, by a suspended chord, by a few notes that serve as an allure; the remainder is completed in the ear of the attentive listener who has become the associate of the artist. Such again is the role of rhythm and measure: "Rhythm and measure," remarks Mr. Bergson, "while permitting us the better to perceive the movements of the artist, make us believe that this time we are the masters of them; the regularity of the rhythm establishes between him and us a sort of union, and the periodic returns of the measure are so many invisible threads by means of which we make the imaginary marionettes move." [9] Briefly, the multiplicity of the elements introduced by the artist in a work of art is the function of an effect to be produced, of an interest to be aroused in a human being called upon to contemplate it.

VARIETY

For the same reasons, artistic variety must be challenging, and must be clearly expressed. Monotony lulls to sleep the attention of the mind and of the senses. Now, without attention there is no perception of art, and without perception there is no aesthetic pleasure. In the hands of the artist the technical procedure confers on the different parts of the work a distinct prominence and directs their convergence toward the central idea or the principle of unity. In the *Descent from*

---

such as advertisement, style, the faith of a guide, as the asterisk of a Baedeker? These conventional enthusiasms do not enter into the scale of artistic emotions.

[9] *Données immédiates de la conscience*, p. 9.

the Cross by Rubens, the personages contribute, each in a different way, to the taking down of Christ; in the *Florentine Wrestlers,* each member of those athletic bodies participates in its own manner in wrestling. In the drama the secondary actors set in relief the principal hero, and the accessory facts emphasize the fundamental plot. It is by this same attention to variety that the painter fills in his background, multiplies his colors, disposes his lights and shadows, and makes room for occasional details. Let us borrow another example from music, the art so profoundly human, and from the procedure J. S. Bach follows in his classical *Fugue.* This is composed of two fundamental melodies which the artist develops in a multitude of ways, the theme and the counter-theme. But between the two is placed an intermediary, a pause, which the technical terminology calls *divertissement.* *Divertissement,* yes that is what it is; its function is to make a diversion, to divert the attention momentarily, to refresh it, to bring it back later more vigorously to the primitive melody. The trills, the arpeggios, the chords, the dissonances, the fantastic designs, the other particularities of the concert or of the sonata have no other aesthetic function than to afford a respite, to rest the hearer, and to prepare him for new musical ideas.

Of all the procedures which produce artistic variety, there is no more powerful one than contrast, or the diversion leading up to the opposition of elements; contrast of characters, of situations, of emotional appeal in literature, contrast of instrumental qualities; contrast of light and shadow, everywhere the aim pusued is the same: to render more brilliant an idea the artist wishes to express. It is to contrast that Rembrandt attributes his most powerful effects. Sometimes, as in the *Night Round,* the master floods the expressive features of the faces with luminous rays, making them fairly gleam from the dark background of the picture. As one gazes from the farthest distance at the extremity of the long galleries in the Amsterdam Museum, the eye focuses on the expressive group of night-rovers. Sometimes by an inverse procedure, evident in this artist's portraits, the luminous rays light only one side of the face, and under a wide-rimmed hat the design of the eyes is merely hinted, and you are obliged to look for them. But by fixing your attention you meet the glance, and suggestion does the rest. Is not the eye the mirror of the soul? Long ago Plotinus advised painters to concentrate on the eyes for the whole effect of their technique.

Whatever is true in the theory of "ugliness surmounted" is explained by the same law of value: ugliness may serve as a foil and under this title it ceases to be ugly. St. Augustine assigned such a role to cosmic evil; badness, by contrast, makes the good appear brighter and, thanks to his theory, the economy of the universe becomes richer (*luculentior*). The bad, the ugly, the gloomy are not beautiful in themselves but in the measure to which they arouse man's perceptive faculties and put into relief the fundamental elements of the work of art.

Unity

With unity, the main quality of the artistic order, as of all order, are connected other phenomena no less interesting.

The elements, varied and multiple, which enter into the composition of a painting, of a statue, of a cathedral, or of a concerto, of a poem or of a novel, would be only chaos if a principle of unity did not inform them and make them coherent. Only on condition that they hold together, do they acquire a value and meaning. To evolve with intensity the idea which is the unifying principle of the work, to make a powerful impression on the hearer or the spectator, such is the secret of the masters; the more powerfully the idea is represented, so much the more does the work achieve beauty. The principle of unity is nothing but the idea or the system of ideas, chosen by the artist, which he has desired to express, to render startling, by all the means at the disposal of his chisel or his palette, by his marshaling of sounds and of words. With penetration Sully Prud'homme remarks that each art has its ideas. There are not only literary ideas, but there are architectural ones, as, for example, Gothic lines; there are musical ideas, such as melodies; there are sculptural ideas, such as attitudes of the human body, and pictorial ideas as expressed in design and coloring.

All the domains of sensible reality are open to the artist in this choice of the principle of unity. Recalling a division referred to farther back, we note that this principle will be of a static or of a dynamic order. The work is of the static order if it puts in relief what a thing is or is intended to be. It is of the dynamic order if it sets forth a function or an activity, indeed, even a utility which the artist has rendered significant.

To find examples of this we need only open at any page the large book of the history of art. An important group of Ionian sculptors undertook the transforming of the human body into a sort of impassibility. The principle of unity to which they adhered was that of plastic regularity; it was made to stand forth in a great number of ways: you may recall all those busts of young men and of goddesses, those Apollos, those Venuses, whereon the sculptors have intentionally rectified the lines of the nose, aimed at absolute symmetry in all the members. No emotion, either sweet or violent, touches these mouths of marble. "This art," says Winckelmann, "is like pure water which is the better so far as it has neither odor nor taste." But there are other groups of antique statuary. There is, for example, *The Dying Gaul* of the Capitol where the eloquence of the marble expresses magnificently the collapse of a body, supple and vigorous; or there are the *Florentine Wrestlers* where the triumph of physical force appears in clear light. Two athletic bodies with muscles distended appear to rain telling blows. One of them, the conqueror, raises his arm in the attitude of a man prepared to strike with full force. Here the principle of unity is not, as referred to previously, of a static order, but of the dynamic. The artist has chosen wrestling as a dominating ideal, a corporeal activity; or again, as in the *Laocoön,* and Michelangelo's *Pietà,* it is internal emotion which the exterior movement reveals.

In proportion as the mind seizes the elements of the work, it brings them under the sway of the controlling ideal of the artist; progressively the network becomes complicated, the variety of relations between parts multiplies; the richness of the order lies revealed, and the soul is flooded with delight.

Unity established in multiple and varied proportion forms the foundation for the beauty of compositions of design; and the artist has an illimitable choice in subjects of the static order (flowers, arabesques) or of the dynamic (living episode.) When the design is in color, the order represented acquires a new attraction. The symmetrical arrangement of the personages around a center (as, for example, in Rembrandt's *Lesson in Anatomy,* in Rubens' *Descent from the Cross*) or in the form of a square (Corregio's *The Holy Family*) is a further means of achieving unity in a design; the coloring of the details and of the whole is another. In Rubens' *Descent from the Cross* the livid body of Christ, lying on a white winding cloth, is the central subject to which all the personages give prominence, from the workman leaning against the cross to the weeping Virgin.[10]

If from plastic art we pass on to literature, the field of the order is enlarged, for the writer has not only the power of describing beings at rest (order of coordination) and of representing attitudes and exterior actions, but he has the privilege of introducing us into the domain of moral activities and of creating there situations that plastic art is powerless to por-

[10] See also Fromentin's excellent commentary on the Van Eyck brothers' masterpiece, *The Adoration of the Lamb. Op. cit.,* pp. 124 ff.

tray. It is thus that the character of a hero is the principle of unity in the dramas of Racine. "Everybody knows the sublime theme of the tragedy of *Horace;* that he should die. I ask someone who does not know Corneille's play and who has no idea of the ancient Horace, what he thinks of this plot, 'that he should die.' It is evident that the one whom I am questioning, not knowing what this is 'that he should die,' will answer me that to him it appears neither beautiful nor ugly. But if I tell him that it is the answer of a man consulted on what another should do in the combat, he begins to perceive in the reply a sort of courage which does not permit him to believe that it is always better to live than to die, and the 'that he should die' begins to interest him. If I add that it is a question of combat for the honor of his country; that the combatant is the son of the one being questioned; that he is the only one left to him; that the young man had a settlement to make with three enemies who had already taken the lives of two of his brothers; that the old man is speaking to his daughter; that he is a Roman; then, the response 'that he should die,' which was neither beautiful nor ugly, is ennobled as I unfold the account with the circumstances, and it ends by appearing sublime." [11]

We find both the static and the dynamic order in music and in architecture. Tonality is like a fabric on which melody is embroidered; it requires a system of unity which is a means of the listener's entering into himself; and the binary or ternary rhythm rules the development of the melody as the

[11] Diderot, *Œuvres philos.,* II, 141 (ed. Belen, 1818).

arterial pulsation governs the circulation of the blood. They are incomparable factors of unity. These factors, whose resources the classicists have utilized, lend themselves to combinations indefinably new.

"Architectural works (the cathedral, bank, depot, city home, and country home) borrow first of all their unity from their functions and their purpose," which, as we will mention in the next conference, is the whole *raison d'être* of a building;" but this ultimate end is marked by a system of linear forms, which renders it immediately recognizable." The basilicas and cathedrals are not merely any haphazard assemblage of walls and arches, of columns and pillars. Principles guide the eye and enable the beholder to recognize the unity of the edifice. In a Byzantine church this principle is the cupola. On all sides the circular lines direct the eyes toward its radiant majesty; and elegant modulations (such as pendentives and the drum) assure the transition from the square or the octagon to the rounded forms. In a Gothic cathedral the basic principle of unity is the pointed arch which sustains both the small and the large vaulted roofs and permits the sudden rising of the walls, forming the whole system of pillars and buttresses. The Gothic style is a logical coordination; so also are the Roman style and that used in the Greek temples and in the mosque. In all the classic styles a unity of linear coordination dominates the architectural work and tends to achieve the ultimate purpose of the edifice." Thus unity is the cohesive force coordinating all elements in a work," whether a short lyric poem or a tragedy of Corneille, a common-life picture

from Van Ostade or a triptych of Van Eyck, the Sainte
Chappelle, or the cathedral of Amiens.

On the other hand, when an element or a group of elements fails to fit within the unifying pattern, then we have
an aesthetic monstrosity, or ugliness. Therefore in a drama or
in a novel an incoherent character is ugly. That is why the
open-work Gothic monument in the *Mesquita* of Cordova
is an artistic blunder. If in the group of the *Florentine
Wrestlers* which we previously mentioned, the left arm of the
conqueror were left dangling by the side of his body instead
of being tensed in the muscular effort, the work of the Greek
sculptor would be devoid of logic and hence of beauty. The
artist chooses in complete independence the unity which he
intends to implant in his art and the means to realize it; but
once the choice is made he must remain faithful to it. Thus
is explained why the same materials may inspire different
artists in the most varied works,[12] and why one of the magnificent figures of Veronese's *Supper* would be out of place
in a similar painting of Leonardo da Vinci. Here we see a
group of children frolicking on the market place of Blidah in
the Orient. The painter who is inspired by this scene, observes Fromentin, can place himself at different points of
view: "Are the children playing in the sun? Or, is it a sunny
place in which the children play? The question is not useless." [13]

[12] See below, chap. 5.
[13] "Une année dans le Sahel, Blidah," *Revue des deux Mondes,* September,
1858.

These reflections lead us to consider a series of procedures used in the production of a work of art in order to accentuate its unity and better to establish it. There is, first of all, the subject. The picturesque or historic fact fixes the attention powerfully on the content. The literary or plastic subject matter, the theme of the musical composer, the local color with which the painters and writers mark their works, are dependent on the artistic value or the power which they possess in augmenting the connecting links or in the coherence of the elements.

A work of art achieves its unity not only by being coordinated within itself but also by asserting its individuality in the face of its surroundings. It gains by its isolation; standing apart, it holds the attention of the spectator to the exclusion of all else. The framework in which a painting is placed, with its brilliant or dull-colored gildings, with its flat or rounded molding, is not an indifferent accessory, a passe partout meant to receive interchangeable pictures. The frame of the painting is the prolongation of the work and the guardian of its individuality. It is that which, on the panel of the parlor salon, isolates it from the surrounding objects whose close proximity might spoil its effect. Hence in art exhibitions the paramount question is about the place where the picture will be placed. Likewise nothing is more difficult than classification from the artistic point of view of the many works assembled in the same museum. The place of honor is always a place out of line like the one occupied by the *Venus de Milo* in the center of the salon at the Louvre, which brings out so

well the white lines of the body of the goddess against the
somber orange-red of the velvet.

The Splendor of Beauty

Let us conclude: artistic order owes its beauty to the
splendor with which it adorns itself and to the extent to which
it provokes contemplative joy in the subject whom it inspires.
It is suited to man's capacities. In the commentaries on the
treatise called the *Divine Names* by Pseudo-Dionysius, the
Areopagite, whose aesthetic enthusiasms bear an Alexandrine
flavor, the philosophers of the Middle Ages discuss a quality
of beauty which is well applied, it seems to me, to the exigencies of the artistic order which they call splendor (*claritas
pulchri*). A work of art makes an idea gleam forth from sensible materials: "*Pulcrum congregat omnia . . . secundum
quod forma resplendet super partes materia sic est pulcrum
habens rationem congregandi.*" [14] The text is from a tract by
Albert the Great written in the thirteenth century. St.
Francis de Sales is manifestly inspired by this teaching when
he writes at the beginning of the *Treatise on the Love of God*:
"The beautiful thing being called beautiful, because its vision
delights, it is necessary that besides union of parts and distinction, integrity, order, and integration, it should possess much
splendor and lustre in order that it be easily seen and recognized; voices to be beautiful must be clear and distinct, discourses intelligible, colors brilliant and resplendent." [15]

[14] *De pulcro* (ed. Uccelli, 1869), p. 29.
[15] *Traité de l'amour de Dieu,* Bk. I, chap. 1.

The work of art must be resplendent: by the multiplicity of its elements, by the variety of the relations uniting them, by the principle of unity cementing them. Only on this condition does the work speak to the soul and fill it with its radiance.

Let us add that art, being a human creation, is always imperfect in one respect or another and thus offers room for distinguishing degrees in its beauty. For the same reason, the artistic order is not necessarily true in every respect. Goethe's *Faust* unfolds in an atmosphere of pantheism, a system which militates against sound philosophic reasoning. The artistic order can likewise be immoral, and the question will be asked later on whether the immorality affects its beauty.

It remains to be shown that the beauty of nature like that of art is a function of the order which it displays.

CHAPTER V

The Perception of Art

Two Moments in the Impression

HAVING considered the object of artistic endeavor, we must now study the impression that it produces. Beauty of art consists in a relation of the expressed order to the subject whom it impresses. If you deny that adaptation of the works to the capacities of the subject is necessary, the very principle from which beauty arises disappears, as does the idea of sonship if you refuse to consider the son in relation to the father who begot him. The impression of art is not, therefore, a thing adventitious to beauty, a secondary phenomenon; it is a constitutive element of the beautiful.

In what, then, are we to find that delectable stirring of the soul when it enters into intimate contact with an artistic work? Of what sort is the pleasant psychological disturbance which such a work provokes? The phenomenon that fills

66

aesthetic consciousness has artistic pleasure, the emotion of art, or the enjoyment of art. The impression of art is an appellation that we find more satisfying than any of these latter because it is more comprehensive. The soul receives the imprint of the work; it is captivated, held, and lured into the most intimate communings with its best self. At the first shock, the condition of the soul seems to be that of perfect union with the beautiful thing; but a little attention makes us see that the unison is quickly decomposed into a kind of psychological symphony.

The impression of art admits a double, or even a triple, aspect: at first we perceive the general character of the work, the lines of a monument, the theme of a sonata, the content of a painting, a sculpture, a drama. This is the representative element of the aesthetic experience, which we will call the perception of art. A love and a sympathy accompany this perception, and we unite ourselves with the work. To the extent to which we contemplate it we love it, and the result is a pleasure which in all civilizations has been looked upon as the noblest of joys and the most exquisite of delights. This pleasure in the presence of a work of art is the emotive element of the aesthetic experience.

The perception of art, the emotion of art made of love and accompanied by pleasure, are, I know, elements of the same psychological reality. For all are commingled in the impression by which beauty enraptures us. "The more one descends into the depths of consciousness," we may say with M. Bergson, "the less one has the right to treat the psychological

facts as things which are in juxtaposition." [1] But this view serves to complicate rather than simplify the study of the state of consciousness which fills us on coming in contact with a work of art; it is necessary for our investigation to dissociate things which in reality are closely united and to introduce division, even though unity is restored after the analysis is completed. For didactic reasons and for clearness, we shall try to discover first of all what is implied in the perception of art, and we shall attempt to show in what follows whence arises the emotion that is aroused.

The Aesthetic of Life

But as a preliminary we ought to consider an opinion, cherished by a group of contemporary theorists, one which, if it could be proved, would offset the psychological hypothesis that we propose to establish; those who subscribe to what they call "the aesthetics of life" would reproach us for confining the artistic phenomenon to the first step in the act of knowing. In their opinion all vital impressions of whatever sort are susceptible of becoming aesthetic: the domain of the beautiful is as large as that of life itself. Thus one may ascribe the aesthetic character to organic sensations which fall within the field of consciousness, including vague kinesthetic sensations which inform us about the condition of our bodies. The aesthetic impression becomes identified with the joy of living.[2]

[1] *Données immédiates de la conscience,* p. 7.
[2] "Human life is dominated by four great needs or desires which correspond to the essential functions of material existence: to breathe, to move, to nourish

Here indeed is awkward confusion between the pleasant ✓ and the beautiful. How are we to disprove these gratuitous assertions except by a final appeal to the verdict of humanity. The human language in which this verdict is expressed refuses to attribute an aesthetic character to the lower functions of life. We do not speak of beautiful respirations or of beautiful digestions. After all, these physiological pleasures, so profound, so infinitely more common and more accessible than aesthetic joys, are aroused by contact with nature; they are the joys of well-being, and we have shown, while treating of the beauty of nature, that they are far removed from the aesthetic impression which nature is capable of arousing. Applied to art, these states of physical life may be concomitants of the aesthetic impression and may exercise on it an indirect influence; but they by no means constitute its essence. One who has just had an attack of bad digestion will scarcely relish a visit to a museum; but the healthy and indefatigable assimilative processes of a rustic will not necessarily procure for him the aesthetic enjoyment of a masterpiece. Let us dismiss further discussion of this exaggerated form of an aesthetic of life.

THE ROLE OF THE SENSES

The impression of art has its source in a cognition, or in a perception, that is, in an act by which a person represents to himself a certain object, and this object is regarded as exterior

oneself, to reproduce. We believe that all these diverse functions are capable of taking on an aesthetic character." Guyau, *Les problemes de l'esthétique contemporaine* (Paris: Alcan), pp. 20–22.

to us. Very well. But what perception? Our knowing life admits a numberless and varied acquaintance with reality. Is it
the exterior sensation that generates beauty; or the internal
sensation, principally the constructive imagination, always
more or less overdeveloped in the great artists; or does the
perception of art arise in the intellect, the most perfectly
representative and specifically human power? As a matter of
fact, the perception of art is a complex affair and results from
a harmonious mingling of exterior sensations, imaginative
representations, and intellectual notions. This is the important theory we wish to establish in detail.

The part played by the senses is primary and easy to prove.
Sight and hearing are the two great avenues through which
our artistic impressions pass; in the plastic and musical arts
their function is so fundamental that the explanation needs no
elaboration. "No painting but is a caress to the eyes, no music
but a pleasure to the ear." [3] In fact, painters, designers, and
sculptors are visual types, their eyes delighting in shades,
colors, forms, delicacy of detail and relief which the uninitiated fail entirely to perceive; musicians are auditory types,
and some performers on stringed instruments perceive variations to the eighth of a tone. Every artist is in certain ways a
sensist who obeys exterior sense stimulation as the Eolian
harp the wind; he is fond of variety, and is pained by the inharmonious.

If we take account of the fact that the feeling of the shapes
of things completes and coordinates the visual perception of

[3] Brunetière, *L'art et la morale* (Paris, 1898), p. 29.

positions, we can add that touch, properly speaking, is susceptible of contributing to the formation of artistic perception. With the blind, tactual sensitivity produces wonders, and antiquity has bequeathed accounts of sculptors who, deprived of sight, found beauty in the shape and relief of plastic forms by caressing them with their delicate hands.

It is to sight, to hearing, and to touch, within certain limits, that the sensible impressions which are the generators of beauty may be ascribed. And if I have paused for a while at this traditional and classical thesis, it is in order to encounter anew the so-called aesthetic of life, which, under pretext of letting beauty enter by every door of the soul, claims for the sensations of smell and taste the same privileges as for sight and hearing. "Perfumes have an artistic character," says Guyau, "and the tastes of liquors and savory dishes are so prolific of the impression of beauty that an art has been constituted out of them, the culinary art, in order to study the effect of their combinations." Let us not delay to show what is inadmissible in this psychology, which places in opposing categories, information of consciousness and linguistic expression. Plato remarks that no one ever spoke of a beautiful odor. It is not sufficient to answer with Guyau, "but we ought to say it."

THE ROLE OF THE IMAGINATION

The feast of the exterior senses is but the prelude of the perception of art, a prelude obligatory but insufficient. To the perceptive role of the visual and auditory sensations is added that of the imagination which completes and intensifies them. I refer to this inner sense in order to demonstrate all that I have said of artistic mutilation, of prevision, of suggestion, and of all these procedures so well known to the artist, thanks to which he arouses in the spectator and the hearer the active work which makes them associates of artistic creation. This reproductive and constructive imagination is what, by way of association, completes the musical themes that the composer, in a given moment, contents himself with suggesting; it is the constructive imagination which, aroused by complementary images, transmits to the entire picture the impression of relief which the contour of the bracelet gives to the arm; it is what fills the emptiness intentionally introduced in their works by poets or novelists. More rarely it supplies for the defect of a sense (as with Beethoven when, in spite of his deafness, he composed his last symphonies). Its chief function in the perception of art is to intensify colors, designs, forms, and sounds. Its power of augmenting the impression has been compared to an electric current which runs through the filament of the electric bulb; the platinum thread is formed of thin spirals which, as soon as given incandescence by the closing of the circuit, appear to thicken and become enlarged.

The Role of the Intellect

Lastly, it does not suffice, in the enjoyment of art, to apply merely our senses and imagination: there is required what is most elevated in our cognitive power: the mind. I should like to show the importance of this faculty, whose intervention in the perception of art is too often disregarded, although it alone puts us in contact with the ideal that the artist has placed in the work.

In the cathedral of Le Mans is a chapel for relics, which glassmakers in the first half of the thirteenth century decorated with marvelous glass reliquaries. In the splendor of iridescent colors the medallions portray twelve or fifteen Gothic Virgins carrying the infant God in their arms. It would be difficult to find side by side in such limited space a larger number of artistic representations of the Mother of God. Now, although they have come from the same workshop, reflect the same style, and treat the same subject, one is surprised at the individuality of expression in each of these small figures.

Besides the wall paintings found by Rossi in the catacomb of St. Priscilla, which archaeologists say date back to the fourth century, the frescoes, paintings, designs, and reliefs, sculptures and statues, consecrated to the Blessed Virgin, are to be counted in the hundreds of thousands. No subject seems able to tempt artists more. It is their Madonnas that constitute the most beautiful gems in the artistic garland of Lucca della Robbia, of Bellini, of Memlinc, of Raphael, and of Murillo. Here we are shown a glorious Virgin, radiant in her maternity; there the Mother of Mercy, full of an anxious solicitude and revealing a sad foreknowledge of sorrow. Here the woman and the mother tenderly expressive of the whole scale of human sentiments, there the predestined creature, interposed between heaven and earth, the inspired victor, the perpetual mediatrix, in which the gesture both implores and protects. Now, do you not see that it is an abstract idea we mean when we say of a statue of the Blessed Virgin that it expresses piety, grief, grace, majesty, or that its body is the imprint of elegance? Sorrow, grace, majesty, elegance, radiance, maternity, and so on are realities which speak to the abstractive faculty of the intellect. This language the senses do not understand or they grasp it in a different way; between the concrete sensation and the abstract thought there is a difference of nature which we need not demonstrate here but which all spiritualistic philosophies recognize.

The same is true in literature, and I cannot do better by way of proof than to state a few of the clear-cut texts of Aristotle's *Poetics* in which the whole aesthetic of intellectualism is set forth with great clearness. In speaking of tragedy, Aristotle assigns to it as an end "the creation of types" (*Poetics*, XV, 13); and he gives this remarkable definition of poetry: "It has for an end the giving of proper names to generalities" (IX, 3). Place a proper name in an abstract type, and you have what the glass blowers did in Le Mans. Is not this what Molière did in his masterpieces? It is the type of the avaricious man, that is, the idea of avarice which we contemplate in the concrete traits of Harpagon. We can easily see that this conception extends to every literary form: through the episodes which furnish the plot of the action, the novelist depicts characters and sentiments that put us in the presence of universal ideas; the entire art of the novelist consists in the spreading out of a procession of data, real or imagined, of the everlasting movements of the human soul.

Because no image of the Mother of God exhausts the idea or the group of ideas that are implied in maternal love, the same artist, Raphael, for example, was able to paint various Madonnas. The same abstract ideas of sorrow, of plastic regularity, of suffering, of sacrifice, of devotion to one's country, of pleasure, of piety, or of struggle may be presented in a countless number of productions. That is how whole periods in the history of art have been made to live again from a small number of artistic subjects, of genuine themes, in the studios; and no more striking example of this could be cited than religious painting from the time of Giotto until the seventeenth century. Historians record that two books have furnished the subjects for nearly all the great paintings: the *Golden Legend* written by the Dominican, Jacques de Voragine, and the *Meditations on the Life of Christ* by an anonymous Franciscan.

On the same typical model nature multiplies individuals, and on each of these productions she imposes a stamp of individuality. No two oaks in the forest are alike; in the millions of persons constituting a people no two bodies and two souls are alike in every respect. Now, has not the artist the power to create diverse images of the same type, to represent the oak or the man under varied and clearly individualized forms, to realize the concrete where the intelligible element is intimately united with the designs and the sounds, conformable to the ideal which presides in every artistic execution?

Hence art is justly called "the grandson of God." We have already commented on this declaration of Aristotle which answers so well the peripatetic and scholastic ideology of the Middle Ages: "Poetry (and one can say all works of art) is something more philosophical and more serious than history, since poetry concerns itself especially with the universal, and history with the particular."[4] From this we understand that in works of art the individual and the abstract do not exclude each other; they coexist and intermingle.

We must go still further: the work of abstraction is clearly evident, not only in the arts of imitation, but also in architecture and music. The recalling of an architectural design and of variations of its visible motifs furnishes the mind with the materials from which one abstracts the form. Therefore simple linear designs, such as the semicircle and the ogive arcs, or the more complicated, as the curved arch of the semicircular vault, and the crossed ogives, are the principles of unity which speak much more to the mind than to the eyes. It is the same in music, where the melody and the rhythm of a work are so well abstracted by the intellect that we produce the variations which the artist has made subordinate.

These considerations show at the same time how vast is the sphere over which the control of the intelligence extends. The word "abstraction" causes fear to untold partisans of intellectualism who repudiate it for lack of understanding. Abstraction is a primordial function of the mind by which we envisage any element of reality, corporeal or incorporeal, phys-

[4] *Poetics,* IX, 3.

ical or moral, apart from all of the conditions of the particularity in which it is enveloped. By way of abstractive power we perceive maternity or avarice in the same way as we distinguish the Roman arch in the Notre-Dame Cathedral and the theme of a fugue in a work in Bach. This thought brings us back by the psychological route to the doctrine that we have met before in the metaphysical point of view (each art has its ideas; it lives by them.)

These ideas afford a plastic and moral content in sculpture, in painting, and in the arts of design. In architecture the intellect feeds on linear ideas. In music the ideas are melodies, In the music of J. S. Bach, which is at the same time the most intellectual and the richest, we have no difficulty in detecting the themes, the design, the fundamental rhythm of a work the great artist knew how to put into exquisite form with consummate art. But it is literary ideas that are the most numerous because literature can translate all the aspects of the physical and the moral world into a language of images wherein the exterior senses furnish the material.

OTHER PROOFS

A new order of consideration will show the value of the role of intelligence in the perception of art and will yield us a second argument in favor of the intellectual theory. It can be summarized thus: there is a considerable group of artistic productions which acquire sense only if we understand their end: moreover, all the work of the artist consists in rendering this end clear and brilliant to the eyes of the mind. Such is the case with architecture and the industrial arts. The construction of city dwellings or of country homes, of banks and of railroad stations, of temples and of cathedrals answers their purpose and utility so well that, if you should suppress these ends, the edifices would no longer have their *raison d'être*. They would no longer exist. He was right who defined architecture, as the clear expression of a satisfied need. To show clearly the use, the utility, that is, the order of finality, of an edifice, is the formula from which arises the secret of its beauty. These finalities are many and varied. There are some general ones: every edifice having to spread over and shelter a certain space is necessarily made up of parts which support and parts which cover, and, as it must be lighted, the designer must reserve room for openings which give access to the light. Schopenhauer has written some worth-while pages on these dynamic functions of materials, and he points out that the beauty of the edifice grows in proportion as the functions of the support and of the weight are rendered in a way more distinct. Thus a vertical wall expresses less clearly its function of support than a pillar or a column; a ceiling gives the idea of weight much less than does a vaulted roof. The general functions of architecture are perfected by the proper ends of the edifice. That is why a city home is not built like a villa in the dunes, or a station like a cathedral. A staircase reveals an aesthetic character when it suggests ascending motion, as does the visible staircase of the John Beauce hotel; and in one village of Flanders there is not even a rectory but which, by its modest and discreet air, discloses its designated purpose.

We will complete the establishment of what we believe to be the true principles of architectural beauty by recalling that the end of the edifice and its parts may be made brilliantly clear by most diverse means. The linear coordination is directed to the end or purpose; but it is susceptible of giving rise to styles indefinitely varied. Gothic art is not more beautiful than Roman art; it is simply different. Both express in distinct formulas the *raison d'être* of these lofty temples of stone that men raise to the glory of God.

In the course of a visit to the cathedral of Amiens, an archaeologist among my friends invited me to climb to the top of the edifice in order to observe the angular character of the keystones of the vaulted arch of those admirable transepts of the choir which are classed among the most elegant of Gothic art. I could then read in the stone the chief function entrusted to it: to hold in a perfect equilibrium the thrust of the seven arches of the vaulted roof, and when again from below I viewed the marvelous nave, a clearer perception of its purpose increased rather than lessened my artistic gratification.

By an inverse phenomenon, the irrational, the want of harmony, between a form and an end, are sources of displeasure, because they break the purposive unity of the edifice. Let a person place upon the keystone such ornamentation as would make more evident to the eyes and to the mind its role of master stone. Nothing better. But let him change this decoration to ornate pendentives representing scenes of the Crucifixion or such as would be represented in the Gothic art of the sixteenth century, and nothing is more unaesthetic. I will say the same thing about columns if, instead of giving the impression of supporting something, they look as though they were suspended from the ceiling of the churches, or were being crushed by the edifice. These examples are sufficient to show that in certain arts the end manifested by means of linear forms is the principle which unifies the work. The study of the industrial arts would give us other applications of the same law.

But if this is the case, then the intervention of the intellect is manifest. Finality is in fact perceptible only through intellectual activity. It supposes a network of relationships between the means and the ends, and the perception of these relations brings into play a complex system of abstract ideas. Thus we see how difficult it is to deny the intellectual character of the perception of art.

We could add that, if objective beauty comes from order, from the action of the intellect alone arises its perception, and therefore without the entry of intellectual activity on the scene there is no artistic impression. The precise moment when I perceive at least a modicum of the order spread about in nature is the moment when I realize its beauty: and the aesthetic impression differs on no other basis from the impression it gives of beneficence.

Let us finally remark, by way of one more argument in favor of our thesis, that certain arts, in addition to the artistic impression, produce some impressions foreign to beauty. Music furnishes an example when it serves to put children and even grown-ups to sleep, when it facilitates digestion, when it sustains the energies of a marching regiment, or otherwise exercises a sedative or tonic influence foreign to its artistic effect.[5] What differentiates the first from the second is the absence of a part, and the presence of another part of the perception of the musical idea and of the principle of order which binds them together.

To summarize: the perception of art takes rise in visual and auditory sensations, whose data are completed and intensified by the imagination; and it is from these concrete data that the intellect formulates the idea or the ideas that the artist has placed there.

ART AND THE SCIENCES

This triple perceptive activity should not be regarded as a sort of mosaic of states of consciousness. It constitutes a harmonious whole, a contemplative ensemble, and ends in a unique action. This character of the perception of art will point the way to a distinction between art and science. Let us take, for example, one among the innumerable masterpieces that are representations of the Virgin. Let us consider, if you

---

[5] Thus, as we have already said in a previous study (*La valeur esthétique de la moralité dans l'art*), the number of those who enjoy music without understanding it is considerable. The musical forms develop a high degree of nervous excitement, and many are satisfied with the pleasant lulling into which they plunge the senses. Among those who frequent the theater, many ask nothing beyond a rapturous sort of drowsiness. This state of passive sensibility is not artistic. A person in that state, hearing productions of diverse individuality, does not distinguish. On the contrary, in one who listens to music as an artist would, there is nothing resembling this passivity; he reacts to what he hears and enters actively into it.

wish, Raphael's *Sistine Madonna,* that graceful and smiling lady with deep-set eyes who carries her infant in the folds of her mantle. Our perception is not made of three distinct and superimposed acts, the first, as it were, in which we see the form and colors, the second where the imagination recognizes the reliefs of the figure, the profundity of the eyes, the perspective of the drapery through which there are visible the lines of the Virgin's body and of those of the two persons who contemplate her; and finally the third, whereby from these contours we gather the ideas of youthfulness, of grace, of gravity, and of sweetness. Quite the contrary: we contemplate the content of our ideas, the ideas of a loving and happy mother, in the habiliment of the sensible forms in which they are wrapped; intellectual contemplation is nourished on these attitudes, colors, designs, and ideas which individualize the artistic ideal of Raphael's *Madonna.* That is why the perception of art lives, when all has been said, in an intuition, the intuition of the abstract in the particular. Raphael did not make a painting of the maternal love of the Virgin; he imagined a figure of a woman with an expression of special traits, placed in such an attitude, in such designs; there then results such a *Madonna* and not another.

It is otherwise with a work that nourishes the intellect in the acquisition of science. Here the contribution of the senses is only the experimental material in which the scientist tries to discover that which is. When the chemist subjects chlorine to reactions in the laboratory in order to discover its mode of activity, it matters little to him whether such particles of chloride or some others furnish the matter of experiment; the law alone concerns him. In the same way, our notion of avarice, or of maternal love which as the object of knowledge has entered the treasury of moral ideas accumulated from our experience, has for us a signification detached from any particular miser, and from such or such a loving mother.

At the moment of the perception of art we are not conscious of the work operating in us; we do not analyze the procedure which makes us contemplate the brilliancy of the abstract idea in the individual and in the concrete data of sense or of imagination. Spontaneously the intellect yields itself to the work, it submits to its domination, and it is delighted to the extent to which it forgets itself and is unaware of the method of its activity. When it reflects on the process, when it asks itself how it is progressing in the presence of the work of art, the charm is broken, the aesthetic attitude has ceased, and the psychological work begins. The intellect in the perception of art does not go beyond the contemplation which constitutes its activity in the field of percept and concept. Nothing in this activity resembles the work of decomposition which is characteristic of the investigative process.

To explain the intuitive side of the perception of art, as well as its superiority over sensation, must we resort to a new and special mode of knowledge, a kind of mysterious delusion? It does not seem so to me; the ordinary resources of representative life suffice here, on condition that we admit this close union of sensation and concept in the single act of contemplation. All is clear in the perception of art; the excitation and the thrill which accompany it arise from the emotion aroused, or the artistic sentiment proper.)

PERCEPTION PROGRESSIVE

Through the interaction of the perceptive faculties, the grasp of the work of art is extensive; it invades our whole consciousness and takes possession of what is most human in us. As can easily be gathered from the foregoing, it admits of a degree of intensity, and thus the perception of art passes from one stage to another.

The first, which we have called the aesthetic shock, is the impression of the whole that comes to the spectator or the hearer placed for the first time before a work of art and experiencing the initial agitation which makes him aware of the beauty of the work. This is an all-pervading impression, which puts one's whole perceptive being in an expectant attitude and leaves an enduring trace in the memory. The first hearing of a symphony of Beethoven, the first visit to the Chartres Cathedral, the first vision of Rubens' *Descent from the Cross,* the first view of the *Venus of Milo* in the Louvre are memorable events for those who know how to live them. After the first cognition the work of further penetration begins: the eye scruntinizes the colors, the forms, the designs, the recesses; the imagination is set into action; one by one the ideas arise, and little by little the perception is enriched. A second, a third hearing of the symphony makes us understand and taste the many details which had at first been overlooked; another visit to the Cathedral brings new discoveries, and so it is with a painting, a poem, or a statue. The more we live in intimacy with the masterpiece, the more it reveals and gives of itself. This is not to say that the perception of the whole disappears and that the work breaks up into detail, but each element newly grasped is incorporated into the integrated order, is made one with what was perceived previously, and acquires an aesthetic meaning through its relation to the whole. The end of the perception of art, the final stage, is found to be the full and harmonious possession of the ideal, embracing all the elements of beauty, and implying the intimate impenetration of the artistic thought, a communion of the soul of the spectator with the soul of the one who invented the sensible forms and concretized them.

INTELLECTUALISM

The philosophy of art to which we subscribe is, as one may see, an intellectualistic philosophy, but of a mitigated intellectualism, since it depends in part on the activity of the senses. It takes account of the perceptive point of view, and this fact sets it strongly at variance with sentimental aesthetics and explains not less well than these the emotive side of the impression, as we will show in the following chapter.

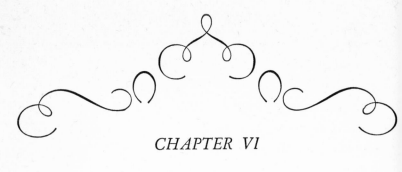

CHAPTER VI

Artistic Emotion

FACTORS OF ARTISTIC EMOTION

THROUGH the first impression, the artistic shock, the work arouses in us a recognition; and as little by little the diffusion of its elements takes place, it completely fills our consciousness. Now at each of its stages, the perception of art is accompanied by an affective state which one commonly calls the emotion of art, or artistic feeling, which ravishes the soul as a feast would gratify the appetite; it is unique. The vocabulary of affective psychology is inexact and uncertain, for the phenomena which it studies take place in a sort of obscure clarity in consciousness. Pleasure and pain are accompaniments of psychological activities, but a state of more or less mystery surrounds both. They place us in the presence of a physical modification so much the more difficult of analysis as the functions of life which they accompany are the more elementary. The joys of health, the organic pleasure which the resurgence of nature in springtime brings to our devital- ized bodies are as hard to understand as the fatigue and melancholy of physiological nature. On the other hand, in- tellectual and moral joys and sorrows, for which one reserves more especially the name of *emotions* in order to distinguish them from physical ones, more clearly reveal their causes, their content, and their effects. In the gamut of feelings or of higher emotions the artistic sentiment is one of those that can best, it seems, be brought out into the open; it is aided to some extent by the light with which the perception of art is sur- rounded. It receives this light by reflection. The emotion or sentiment of art—the two appellations are synonomous— lends itself, in effect, to a disintegration similar to that of the rays of the sun issuing from a prism. There I find these two factors: a transport of love directed toward the perceived work and a thrill of pleasure with which this transport is accom- panied. Let us study each.

The Transport of Love

A work of art evokes an upsurge of love. Like all love, this carries us toward union with the loved object and makes us revel in its possession. This fact is certain. We love the works of art with all the energy of our soul. We yearn toward them as toward very dear friends. We have our preferences in the museum, in the churches, to which we voluntarily direct our observation, and we impose sacrifices on ourselves in order to visit them. A few years ago, in the course of a journey in

France, a friend found it easy to persuade us to make a detour of fifty miles in order to view again the blazing window of the cathedral of Troyes at the setting of the sun. Even in our homes, where each object of art could find a place only by special permission, where each knick-knack is charged with some memory, we have our preferences; permanent or changeable, it matters little; they are the signs of a real affection.

What is the quality of this love of a work of art? In the first place, it is disinterested; it does not rise from cupidity and is not inspired by the utility of the object. The love of beauty and of utility do not blend. A hungry person loves the food served him because of the good it secures him; a working-man loves a good tool on account of the services it renders him; the property owner who covets a near-by field takes pleasure in enlarging his possessions. In all these instances the object is loved with a love of utility, and this does not exist without the possession, more or less exclusive, by the beneficiary. There is nothing like this in the love of a work of art. I do not plan to acquire for my profit or subject to my usage a painting which I admire in a museum. What artist will harbor the idea of rendering himself proprietor of a cathedral? Certainly the joy of a collector cannot be placed above that of the artist, but the two feelings are distinct, and the first excludes the second during the whole time in which it absorbs the mind. Besides, it is not the first which is most noble. Unsociable amateurs, who jealously enjoy their works of art and reserve to themselves the monopoly of enjoyment are madmen by whom the

artistic impression, pure and serene, appears to me to be seri-
ously compromised. Whatever Guyau says to the contrary in
his *Problems of Contemporary Aesthetics,* usefulness is not
beauty. The market places of Paris are not beautiful because
of the quality of useful objects found there in the full baskets
of savory peaches or of delicious peas; and the sensual attraction that can be felt by the gourmet at the sight of so many
good things to eat does not find place in the scale of artistic
sentiments. You will here recognize again the insufficiency of
the aesthetic of life, which throws everything into confusion
in wishing to enlarge immoderately the dominion of beauty.
Certainly—and it is an argument made worth-while by
Guyau—the carter will call the smooth road beautiful which
does not jolt his vehicle; but the hunter also speaks of the
beautiful furrow where he hopes to find a rabbit: and in the
language of the realtor a beautiful farm is a farm of good soil.
In every one of these cases, the epithet "beautiful" is not of
artistic connotation. To pretend this is to play on words; and
no one is deceived by it any more than he would be into thinking that the word "dog" meant the constellation instead of
the animal.

The love of a work of art is disinterestedness; it is free from
self-love. The greater number of psychologists repeat these
formulas of Kantian origin and they add to them that of H.
Spencer that the love of art is a joy of luxury. Let us not believe that the honor of this discovery belongs either to Kant
or to Spencer. Already the philosophers of the Middle Ages
insisted on the distinction between the beautiful and the use-

ful, and in addition made the most profound distinction between the beautiful and the good. The pleasure of the useful,
they tell us, is attached to the material possession of the thing.
It is "that which pleases"; whereas the pleasure of the beautiful springs from a simple knowledge of the thing, "that
whose apprehension pleases." [1] The formula is that of
Thomas Aquinas. The utilitarian aesthetics is not a new
theory belonging to Guyau, since it appears in the aesthetics
of Socrates. "My flat nose is more beautiful than that of
young Kratobyle," says Socrates, "for it serves me better than
his serves him in the smelling of things."

The disinterestedness of the emotion of art is what bestows
on it its purity and its dignity, and it is this also that explains
the calm and the serenity which the work of art engenders,
the respect which it inspires, and the veneration which surrounds it. The disinterestedness of the enjoyment of art is so
characteristic that it bursts forth even when in the things of
art we contemplate the realization of utility. And that such
is the case, we see in the utilitarian and industrial arts, where
utility is the only *raison d'être* and where consequently the
perception has for its object the effulgence and splendor of
the utilitarian end. So true is this fact that there is ground for
distinguishing between the utilitarian enjoyment which the
possession of an object can give (the fact of living in a house,
for example) and the aesthetic enjoyment that is procured
by the consideration of its habitability.

[1] St. Thomas, *Summa theol.,* Ia IIae, q.27, a.1.

The Love of Art

The love of truth afforded by science is a love of security. Doubt is a torment. When the doubt bears on moral questions, like the question of whether God exists or if there is a future life, it becomes a torture. To read the cries of anguish which this doubt drags from the soul of Jouffroy makes one shudder. Certitude, on the other hand, brings assurance; we love the truth since it teaches us of reality in giving us awareness of the agreement of our thoughts, of our judgments, and of our scientific interpretations with reality.

Is the same to be said of the beautiful? No. When we are carried toward the work of art we do not wish to acquaint ourselves with the existence of laws that govern the real or to enjoy the satisfaction that this knowledge procures. Thus the love of the work of art differs from the sentiment which sustains the scholar in the ardor of his scientific researches.

Would there be hidden here, by chance, a love of ourselves, a complacency in finding ourselves in the work, in confiding to it our secret thoughts or our inmost feelings, in projecting our own soul into it? Not at all. It is not we who pour our ego into the work of art: on the contrary, it is the work which fills us with itself, which invades our consciousness with its ideal and expressive content. This is so true that the more the soul yields to the attraction of the work and allows itself to be dominated by the work, the less attention it pays to itself, to such an extent that there comes a moment when the consciousness of its activity escapes it. The most perfect works of art, the most objective and the most intellectual (for example, Greek statuary, the *Divine Comedy*, the Gothic cathedrals, the tragedies of Racine), are also the most resistant to these autoprojections; new proof that the love of art has for its direct object the work loved and not the subject loving. Assuredly it is to the effect on us that the work points as to its final outcome, since every conscious state is our conscious state; and from this point of view we could say that we find ourselves indirectly in the work of art. But this search and this discovery of self is neither the principle of our attraction toward beauty nor the end to which it is directed. To reduce the love of a work of art to the love of self would be to fall into the aesthetic errors of *Einfühlung*, which we will discuss farther on, and to fail to recognize the value of the technique and the primordial role of the work in the impression which it produces.

Let us remember, however, that if the phenomenon of the sentimental projection of the self into things of beauty is not the artistic event properly so called, it is none the less real, and thus is related to affective psychology. That a *Madonna* of Raphael, or a ballad of Chopin should become the confidant of our joys and of our sorrows, of our enthusiasms and our illusions, is a strange effect of art; but at certain periods in our life it can become more powerful than the artistic impression itself. It forms a part, like respect, admiration, or sympathy, of a group of associated feelings which are aspects of love, but are only accompaniments and accessories of the aesthetic sentiment. Several chapters might be devoted to a study of these multiform sentiments which compose the procession of the artistic emotion and which many people confuse with it.

A LOVE OF CONTEMPLATION

What is the nature of the love of a work of art, since it has nothing of the utilitarian or interestedness, and does not consist in a love of ourselves? We may answer: it is a love of pure contemplation. We love the work in order to contemplate it; we rivet our eyes, our ears, our imaginations, our intellects, on ideas, musical, architectural, literary, or plastic, which stimulate our interest by their splendor and joy, which the artist has been able to make shine forth from the material object. Our whole being is attracted by the powerful affirmation of the idea. It is pure intuition of the abstract in the concrete which we cherish, and love finds nourishment continually renewed in proportion as we penetrate more and more the inner recesses of the ideal. The good pursued is the good of contemplation.[2] On this rests the union which we contract with the work of art: a serene and profound union which arouses the soul without agitating it, and which imposes silence on the cupidity of the passions and makes the mind live the most exquisite kind of life.

THE PLEASURE OF ART

After the rush of enthusiasm comes the possession; after the desire, the repose of enjoyment. Satisfied love engenders

[2] "Contemplatio spiritualis pulchritudinis vel bonitatis est principium amoris spiritualis." *Ibid.*, q. 17, a. 2.

delight. The union with the loved work in the act of serene contemplation fills the soul with a special exaltation, which, according to Keats, makes the work of art a source of permanent joy: "A thing of beauty is a joy forever." [3] It is the artistic pleasure properly so called.

In what does this pleasure of art consist, this thrill of enjoyment? The contemporary psychologists who have studied especially the tonalities of pleasure and of pain recognize their inability to define these states of consciousness which Plato had already spoken of in the *Phaedo* through the mouth of Socrates: "How strange a thing is pleasure, my friends, and how near it comes to pain, called its contrary!" The clearest of the results produced by recent researches is the exact statement of the connection between the physiological and the psychological aspects of pleasure and of pain.

Under its extreme form the physiological theory, defended by Lange and William James, reduces all the phenomena of the emotional life to organic disturbances, and the emotions are with them only a form of these bodily commotions. Instead of saying in the common sense manner: I am sad and I cry, one would have to say: I cry, and that makes me sad. William James wished to entend this explanation not only to physical pleasure and pain, but to the delicate feelings among which the artistic emotion holds the first place. "A glow," he writes, "a pang in the breast, a shudder, a fulness of the breathing, a flutter of the heart, a shiver down the back, a moistening of the eyes, a stirring in the hypogastrium, and a

[3] Keats, *Endymion,* Bk. I, p. 164 (ed. E. Rhys, Everyman's Library).

thousand unnamable symptoms besides, may be felt the moment the beauty *excites* us." [4] More than that, he has declared that emotion is a stranger to the pleasure of art and that
this latter resides entirely in a judgment of truth. No matter
what value it has in a case of physiological pleasure or pain,
this theory of James is not applicable to aesthetic emotion and
to the higher sentiments in general. The enjoyment of art is
not an accessory phenomenon which unfolds itself in parallel
lines with the perception of the work: both are integral parts
of a unique phenomenon which is the impression itself, and
which has a right to the same title. The fact is not taken here
into consideration that one cannot reduce the judgment
which accompanies the aesthetic feeling to a simple judgment
of truth, without misrepresenting the facts and confounding
art and science. Besides, in the greater number of cases, the
emotion of art is calm and serene, as in the representation, and
when I enjoy the elegant ogives of the cathedral of Poitiers,
I feel nothing that resembles "a flash of lightning, a stroke on
the breast, a shiver up and down my back." The physiological
concomitant has not, in the production of the pleasure of art,
the predominant role that James assigned to it; its influence
must be reduced to its more exact proportions, and we must
return to the psychological side of the emotion.

Now for the psychological aspect. Must we renounce all
attempt to explain the charm and the pleasure of the impression of art? No. But the study must be made on the only side
which it offers for analysis, that is, in the conscious causes

[4] *Principles of Psychology,* chap. 25 (ed. 1890), p. 470.

which arouse it. What other means, moreover, would there be for speaking of emotion if not in intellectualizing it, in submitting it to the prism of thought and thence converting the thought into a sentiment known or perceived? Thus, in other terms, we are once more brought back to intellectualism, and to the intellectual theory of pleasure. This theory, formulated for the first time by Aristotle, a theory to which one invariably returns, is expressed in a beautiful passage of the *Nicomachean Ethics:* "Pleasure is not the activity itself nor an intrinsic quality of the act, but it is an addition which is never lacking, the last perfection which is added to it, as bloom accompanies youth. Each action has its proper pleasure, and the effect of pleasure is the augmenting of the intensity of the action to which it is attached." [5] Pleasure is to activity what the healthy bloom of complexion is to youth: thus is stated in terms of supreme elegance the principle that pleasure follows upon a conscious activity. The expansion of the organic functions when one feels his vitality surging through him as a beneficent stream, walking, skating, breathing the air while galloping on a fiery horse; the thrill of intense activity, satisfaction of the senses, the pleasure of the eyes at the sight of brilliant colors; the delight of the ear under the caress of melody, the pleasant feel of velvet, the gratification of the palate and the smell, the joys of the imagination and scientific investigation, the moral enjoyment which conscience gives for duty well done: there is not a con-

[5] *Nichomachean Ethics,* Bk. X, chap. 4.

scious activity which cannot become a source of pleasure. On the other hand, without the expenditure of energy there is no pleasure. Inaction engenders only loneliness and lassitude. Even idleness, so prized in warm countries, does not owe its charm to the total absence of activity but to the continual change of activity. A delightful reverie at the fireside after a day of fatiguing labor is not a form of inaction, for the imagination wanders about while the muscles relax. Likewise, without knowledge there is no pleasure: the pleasure of going to sleep is experienced only in the fugitive moment when we feel our nervous and muscular activities relaxing, and it disappears completely when slumber descends upon the vital activity at the threshold of consciousness.

LAWS OF DURATION

Thus is indicated the way to study the psychology of pleasure: it is necessary to determine by what means or under what conditions the expenditure of activity produces pleasure or pain. Since we know by what conscious activities the artistic attitude is produced, the applications to aesthetic pleasure will be readily perceived. These conditions can be formulated into laws, and we shall limit our considerations to three: the law of duration, the law of intensity, and the law of harmony.

The first should not hold our attention long. Just as an excessively long walk causes fatigue and drives away pleasure, in the same way a prolonged visit to a museum becomes boresome, and a too long musical audition exhausts the nerves, irritates the ear, and disperses the most sustained attention. Where moderation is lacking there is no pleasure. Inversely, there is a minimum of duration beyond which interest in the work has not the time to penetrate the mind of the person who should enjoy it. It is manifest also that these limitations of duration between which the activity of contemplation is unfolded in order to generate pleasure, vary according to individual aptitudes and capacities.

LAWS OF INTENSITY

Another law is no less general: the pleasure grows in intensity with the activity which engenders it. To speak only of the activities of perception, a too simple object leaves us indifferent; a too complicated one irks us.

Applied to the pleasure of art, the law shows conclusively that this pleasure increases in proportion as the perception acquires clearness or extends to a more considerable network of relations and of elements. The clearness of the perception engenders, with a minimum of effort and of fatigue, the maximum of activity. Are not the great artists on the violin and piano those whose execution is the most brilliant and clear cut, who excel in giving expression to the minutest details in the musical theme and bringing out with the greatest clarity the thought of the composer? That is what charms us in their talent more even than their virtuosity. For the same reason a work of art that we view the second time pleases more than at the first contact, since we perceive it more clearly, and are cognizant of more of its details. The richer the content of the perception in ordered elements, the more the network of relations which this order implies is extended and enlarged. The more intense also is the activity that we must expend in order to hold the attention in the contemplation, and the greater and more penetrating is the pleasure resulting from it. This is one of the reasons why, in my opinion, the ternary rhythm in music gives more pleasure than the binary rhythm; and the painting which joins color to design, more than the simple pencil drawing. In the same way, as the action in a tragedy becomes more entangled and the intrigue more complicated, the interest rises to a higher and higher pitch.

In the light of this principle we can evaluate the artistic part of archaeology and of history of art, and judge of the aesthetic value of morality.

Art and archaeology do not blend. The enjoyment of archaeology which establishes the origins of the conditions in the civil state, or the history of a statue, and which, with a fragment of marble, tries to reconstruct a whole, is different from that of a painter or sculptor at the moment when he becomes enamored of the beauty of form. But archaeology itself ought to be the vestibule to the temple of beauty. It ought to place itself at beauty's service. "Otherwise," writes a fine critic who is also an artist," the learning that archaeology displays is nothing but trickery. "It has come about that the scaffolding which should enable us to climb up and see better, threatens to prevent us from seeing at all. The purpose of the telescope is not the telescope but the stars." [6]

Thence arises the influence of archaeological discoveries on the perception of art. This knowledge makes for enrichment of that perception by placing the work in a new background of relations. Thus the activity of perception, and thereby the pleasure of art, is increased. It would be difficult to dispute this statement. The metopes of the Parthenon will appear more beautiful to me when my imagination, calling to its service my knowledge of history and Greek archaeology, will in a way bring the work back to its origin and replace it in its environment. Notre Dame de Poitiers appears to me more beautiful when I recall all that pertains to its origin and even to the influence which it has exercised on the evolution of Roman art. And the painting by Brugeois Finsonius, kept in the chapel of the Lyceum at Poitiers, appealed more eloquently to my eyes, to my imagination, and to my intellect when I learned the charming episode which linked its history to that of Flandrine of Nassau. [7]

It is by application of this same principle that a person can best solve the question of whether the morality or immorality of a work of art exercises an influence on its beauty. This is a delicate problem, which is nearly always confused with something else, because it is confounded with this other problem,

[6] A. Kingsley Porter, in an attractive little book entitled *Beyond Architecture* (Boston: Marshall Jones, 1928), p. 23.

[7] This magnificent work representing the *Nativity* was presented to Flandrine of Nassau, abbess of Holy Cross at Poitiers, by her father, William the Silent.

which is also raised about the relation between art and morals and which can be stated thus: Has not art a moral mission to fulfill? The first is of the aesthetic order; the second of the moral or ethical order. Only the first one is our present question.

Before attempting the solution, a correction of the mistaken notion regarding it is necessary. A work of art can produce an effect of morality or immorality, only if, in a direct or indirect manner, it is related to a human act. Thus the nature of things is the decisive factor. Evidently the paintings of Sniedgers representing fruits and flowers have nothing to do with morals. Moreover, the question does not arise as regards all human acts represented in art. Most of the subjects which inspire plastic and literary arts enter this category of actions regarded as indifferent, because their relation to moral good and moral duty does not arise from their sole fact, but depends on a system of media and ends in which the actions are involved and with which the work of art does not concern itself. Bowling and archery, which Teniers has so admirably represented in his scenes of Flemish life, are neither good nor bad in themselves, although they can become one or the other. The farmer who seeks in a game of bowling an innocent recreation does well; the soldier who for the sake of seeing the game would use the time which he owes to military duties does wrong. Hence the impression of morality would be produced by works of art representing positive acts of virtue, such as the heroism of a soldier, a gesture of pardon, an act of adoration, a prayer; just as an immoral work will be such as offends our sense of propriety and decency.

Thus we have isolated from all other questions the question of whether the impression of morality or immorality which the work bears is an asset or an injury to the art.

Now, do you not think that the effect of positive morality —what Taine rightly calls "the benevolence of character"— constitutes an artistic value because it acts on the intensity of the pleasure of the perception? All else being equal, that is, of two works of art equal in finality, in execution, in richness of ordered elements, the one which will present to the aesthetic contemplation a perfect consonance with morality will call for an act of perception more complete, and will engender therefore an enjoyment of art more perfect than that whose subject is destitute of such accord. Murillo's *Saint Francis of Assisi* (Museum of Seville) would surpass in beauty *The Fruit Eaters* (in an ancient picture gallery of Munich) for the sole reason that it shows us the perfect renunciation of a man who embraces poverty. The morality of the work transfigures the purely plastic elements, just as the salute of a soldier exhibits his nobility when we think of the patriotic duty by which it is inspired. There is the secret of the profound impression which is produced even on unbelievers by works like Rubens' *Descent from the Cross* and Velasquez' *Dying Christ*. A noble human being's death on the gibbet is a subject worthy to tempt an artist—but when this crucified one is the God-man, thought pursues the brilliance of the idea of the sacrifice into the supreme region of moral grandeur.

Likewise the triumph of the patriotic sentiment or the duty of paternal affection—which Corneille dramatizes in *Horace* —undoubtedly enriches the artistic order unfolded in the tragedy; and one must say as much of the scenes of *Polyeucte,* of *Cinna,* of *Athalia,* where the spectacle of the most sublime virtue elevates art to its highest summit.

All this confirms the truth that the aesthetic state is made up of activities and of reactions and that in order to judge the work of art, it does not suffice to view it passively. The artist's attitude, far from being a kind of hypnotic condition where personality vanishes, is the placing of a perfect value on the personality.

LAWS OF HARMONY

A third law governs the exercise of the activity of contemplation, the source of the enjoyment of art, and it reaches to depths of the emotional life: the activity must be dispensed in a harmonious manner, for every pleasure is condemned to diminish, even to disappear, when it struggles with pain.[8] A human being is not a sort of mosaic of faculties each acting on its own account and coloring its actions with pleasure or pain. If it were thus, we could suffer in one part of our being without impairing in any way our enjoyment in the other. But as

[8] For the same reason the activity giving rise to the pleasure must be without effort and carried on as a normal unfolding. Shackling of the activity causes unpleasantness, and effort put forth against a resisting obstacle irritates. It is necessary to look in the adaptations of the organ itself for the cause of the pleasure which the eye experiences in following certain curves and colors, and the ear in seizing on certain definite sounds. We may add, with the ancients, that order is pleasing to the intellect because it is itself marvelously ordered: *quia ipsa ratio proportio est.*

a matter of fact, the agent which produces these diverse activities is one: and this unity to which consciousness is a reliable witness brings with it a hierarchy, a subordination in the conscious activities and in the pleasure which they engender. Cry "Fire" in a theater, and this mere threat of being burned and of suffering will cut short the most penetrating enjoyments of the dramatic art. The sight of sorrow is stripped of its bitterness only if one is conscious that this sorrow is feigned, as it comes to us across the footlights. When, seated in a soft armchair, we see before us on the stage a ruffian brandishing his sword, we do not think of running away, and we cry sweet tears at the sad fate of unfortunate heroines. On the other hand, if the sorrow which we are witnessing becomes real, the scene is distressing. Pleasure and pain are emotions of opposite tonality and they cannot dwell together in the same conscious state. The two enter the lists of mortal combat always to the detriment of pleasure.

Now is not one of the shocks encountered in this strife the impression of sensual immorality left by certain works of art? Not that these works are utterly devoid of beauty. The harmony of the forms stands revealed; they have the splendor which the cloak of elegance gives to the artistic idea; to deny them all beauty would be to lack judgment and impartiality. But reason being in man the kingly faculty, that which by nature wounds the moral sense must cause a diminution of the contemplative enjoyment. Immortality in art, which we must not confuse with the nude in art,[9] exercises a negative influence, to the degree to which it disturbs the serenity of con-

[9] By immoral art is meant especially sensual art.

templation. To the same extent it becomes an artistic hindrance. Art has not then for a field the whole of reality, because as soon as the real can no longer produce contemplation in conditions of harmonious enjoyment, the beauty of the work is nullified.

The solutions that have been proposed to this problem are for the most part lacking in logic and are often contradictory. According to Brunetière, all art is immoral because it addresses itself to the senses and all sense pleasure tends to set in play a disorderly movement of the lower appetites. This is sheer error and gross exaggeration. Sense enjoyment is a good in itself; it becomes evil only when it runs counter to the norms set by reason, thereby disturbing psychic equilibrium. Besides, it is evident that a vast category of artistic works are neither moral nor immoral, their perceptible content having no connection with a human act. An opposite error would be to contend that there is no immoral art because art purifies everything, and the artistic forms in which the immoral subjects are clothed annul the impression of immorality in the observers who are attracted by them. This would be true only if the artist were constituted differently from other men.

It can also be said, but to a lesser extent, that the error or falsity by which a work of art is tainted constitutes a hindrance to its beauty. This defect proves a disappointing shock to the human mind hungry for truth, as it offers for the exercise of aesthetic contemplation a view of the world and of life utterly rejected by logic.

Let us close this study of the aesthetic experience by a

consideration that you have doubtless made before and that I shall merely touch upon lightly. Nothing is more thoroughly personal than an emotion, for the pleasure is always my pleasure; and it cannot be otherwise with the delight in the beautiful. The impression of art admits a subjective element, its variability arising from multiple causes, proximate or remote: age, sex, temperament, character, education, social environment, and so on. But we must not therefore conclude that aesthetic impressions are at the mercy of the arbitrariness and caprice of the individual. The pleasure of art is really dependent upon the perception of art, and by it is furnished with the basis of stability. The adage that tastes and colors are not to be accounted for has been wisely corrected by La Bruyère to: "One discusses tastes purposefully." We may add as a corollary, verifiable by experience, that taste is reformable after discussion. The basis for this latter statement is the group of objective elements the artist places in his work, which give to the art a value independent of the circumstances or the environment of those to whom it is addressed. At the conclusion of these studies about the nature of the work of art, we return to the great thesis we expressed at the beginning: the aesthetic phenomenon resides in the perfect harmony between the work and the one who is impressed by it.

CHAPTER VII

Artistic Purpose

INTERNAL AND EXTERNAL PURPOSE

WE have grouped together three questions as problems with which a philosophy of art must deal: What is the genesis of a work of art? What is its nature? What is its final end? The last question remains to be answered: What is the purpose of a work of art?

If by finality we mean the end conferred by the nature of things (the end of the work), we have answered in advance: a work of art serves, and of itself can only serve, to express by sensible means the beauty created by man and fitted to his perceptive and emotive powers. A work of art, like everything else, has for its internal finality the full realization of its nature. It expresses beauty, as fire burns, as an alms relieves. Such is the plausible sense that we can attach to the formula: "Art for art's sake."

But most often another meaning is applied to the end of art. Alongside internal finality, a thing has or can have another end or purpose, superimposed on that of the first in virtue of the will of man; for this reason it is called external, or extrinsic finality. From these extraneous purposes arises the problem of the mission of art. The problem is a complex problem, for we can fix no limitations to the subordinations that the will of man has the power of assigning to his works.

Let us try, while keeping these ends distinct, to arrange them in order. There are two series, the individual and the collective. But the two groups, especially the second, comprise multiple subdivisions. We will note them in passing while stressing by preference the ones that hold a place in contemporary discussion. Each of these many points of view would furnish matter for a special treatise, but their profound study does not belong properly to aesthetics and will find here only a brief treatment.

INDIVIDUAL ENDS

A work of art receives an individual finality as soon as a man assigns to it a part in the organization of his life, as soon as he subordinates it to an ulterior aim other than the expression of beauty. Artistic production and enjoyment enter, therefore, into human conduct in the same way as any other human act does and under this aspect take on a moral character. Moral function is added to the aesthetic function.

The problem of the moral mission of art which appears

thus under a new form differs totally from the one which we considered at the end of the preceding chapter. There it was the case of the aesthetic value of the morality of art, proposed as the object of contemplative perception. Here we consider the moral worth of the aesthetic activity when one subordinates it to ends freely chosen. Now, anyone can see that this second problem, related as it is to morality, ought to be solved according to the principles proper to that science.

In the first place, the subordination of a work of art to some ulterior end cannot in any way harm its character of beauty. The work remains what it is. As in a philosophic or a scientific treatise, the intentions of the author do not affect his field of investigation. "The merit of the artist as artist," writes Thomas Aquinas, "does not depend on the moral dispositions which are his when he executes the work, but on the value of the execution; for the glory of the artificer inasmuch as he is an artificer does not depend on his intentions in making the work but on how good the work is which he makes." [1] "It is not different," he continues, "from the case of the mathematician; provided he works the problem correctly, it is of small importance what his dispositions are while making his demonstration—whether he is sad or joyous."

The value of the work will therefore not be altered from the fact that, for example, the artist yielded to the urge of ambition in carrying out his project, or that he sought, in the sale of his works, the resources required for his material well-being. Strange pretension on the part of certain apostles of

[1] *Summa theol.*, Ia IIae, q.51, a.3.

"art for art's sake" who wish to forbid the artist all other concern but that of producing beauty for beauty's sake, as if the
artist were some sort of misplaced entity prohibited from
directing his own conduct, a waif condemned to abandon
himself, after the manner of a wrecked ship, to chance buffet-
ings on the sea of existence. The work remains what it is, and
in the determination of its value as art the intentions of the
artist do not matter. In the beautiful artistic centuries of the
Middle Ages, image-makers, sculptors, glass-workers, and
miniature-painters were all both artists and promoters of religious fervor. Masterpieces of beauty, their Madonnas were
also messengers of piety. These men worked for the love of
God with religion as one of the great principles which inspired the corporate involvement of so many anonymous
talents. It would be senseless to conclude that their prosody
was vicious on this account or their ideal of art of minor value.
Far from harming the perfection of his work, the purpose of
the artist may constitute a precious stimulus. It was to give
pleasure to Pope Julius II that Michelangelo shut himself up
for several months in the Sistine Chapel. The hope of fame
and the ideal of glorious achievement were able to exercise an
entirely beneficial influence on his talent.

On the other hand, as soon as the production of the work
is viewed not as an artistic fact, but as an achievement of the
free will, it clothes itself in the character of a moral act; and it
then falls under the domain of the laws that govern every
human act, and becomes for the one who contemplates it the

source and the occasion of beneficent or malign effects, of duties and responsibilities, of merit or demerit.

The general principles of individual morality are sufficient to show that, if it is optional for the artist to put his works to the service of an idea or religion or a moral code, we do not well see in the name of what principle he should be obliged to do so. We know the Greek theory of the Socratic period, the cause of the confusion which then existed between beauty and the moral good. It imposed upon the artist the duty of spreading moral ideas among the people. That duty was put into correlation with the social mission of art in the Greek state. The work of art, Plato teaches, is not to be an indifferent distraction but a moralizing agency.

Nothing is more false than this rigorous ethical norm. Since no act of artistic production is the object of a moral obligation, it is necessary to condemn the two theories as equally exaggerated: the one which imposes a moral mission on the artist and the one which prohibits it.

Thence the question of his responsibility is easily settled. The artist is not a privileged being, a superman liberated from the laws that rule the conduct of other human beings. There is no special code which immunizes the artist from the mistakes of other mortals and which makes of his a special caste outside the sphere of humanity. If his work is productive of good, he reaps the benefit; if it produces evil effects, why should he not answer for them? Of the artist whose works are agents of demoralization, we can only say what Pascal said of Montaigne: "His book, not intended to lead men to piety, was not obliged to do so; but one is always obliged not to turn men away from the good." [2]

Artistic apologies for suicide have cost the lives of thousands of men of every age and of every condition; impure art has precipitated into culpable voluptuousness legions of young people. Are not the authors of such sources of evil to be regarded as criminals? [3]

THE CULT OF GOD

Without ceasing to be a continual dispenser of beautiful impressions, a work of art easily becomes, in the intimate life of the individual, a purveyor of consolation, of smiles, of joys, and an agent of moral uplift. It can prove both quieting and strengthening. To the works of art that our homes shelter, to the beautiful familiar objects of our daily life, do we not confide our sorrows in order to alleviate them, our joys to increase them? In the storm of human existence and in the inevitable bruises received along the road of life, a page of literature, an hour of music, an album that recalls the impressions experienced in viewing some masterpieces of art, each drops into the soul a calming influence and offers a soothing diversion that resembles the warm rays of sympathy. In this connection we can bring into service the words of Schopenhauer who calls a halt in the siege of suffering, "an exhilarating beverage

[2] *Pensées* (ed. Havet), p. 344.
[3] The artist is no less the owner of his work. He has over it the right of ownership, and it is proper that the law should protect him against plagiarists and deformers.

which makes one forget the misfortune of existence." The theory is true on condition that it is stripped of its pessimistic tonality. We can transfer to it the optimistic outlook which we profess; for, if pain has a moral significance which enables us easily to justify its presence in human life, and if it is thus reconcilable with happiness, it is nonetheless true that it offers a redoubtable trial to the strongest. Blessed be the work of art which causes at least a momentary cessation of the miseries of life and confers on us new strength and new energy for the struggle!

If this is true, then art is something more than a plaything in the hands of an idler. The Kantian formula of play, adopted and corrected by Herbert Spencer, is acceptable only in one sense, that it expresses the disinterested character of art. Held strictly to the letter, it denies art's serious character, that which constitutes its glory and its strength.

But men have gone much farther than Kant and have attempted to establish a religion of beauty. Some have gone so far as to demand of art a refilling of the void in their souls left by unbelief, to answer to their mystic and spiritual yearnings. The cult of the Supreme Being has been replaced by the cult of art. Man has fallen on his knees before his work and has proceeded to eliminate God in the name of science, and politely to dismiss Him from the world of reality. In the same way man has been willing to reserve to art the homage which belongs only to the Infinite. What an abnormality; as if art by its perfections and imperfections alike did not make us think of the existence of a Supreme Being, infinitely beautiful, and of an order of divine things where beauty is refulgent with a brightness without shadow! In the case of the artist as of others, inordinate pride is indicative of pettiness.

COLLECTIVE ENDS

An agent of moral uplift in the life of an individual, art is even more productive of good in the life of a group. Artistic influence has its brilliant effects on various assemblages of human beings from the most simple, the family and the school, up to the more complicated, such as the city, the nation, and this great family of peoples which is called the civilized world.

Art infiltrates into the family, which is the natural and primordial group; it contributes to the cementing of the links which unite the members. While rendering the knick-knacks of one's apartment things of joy, while putting the touch of elegance to one's furniture, it adds a new attraction to all the other features that make home sweet; it binds a person to his abode. It is not only the artistocrat's mansion which is rendered attractive by beauty, but the modest dwelling of a middle-class worker or of a wage-earner also owns its charm. Much progress is yet to be realized from this point of view. Certain women among the lower classes succeed with small means in giving the home elegance and gaiety, whereas others are wholly incapable of making their surroundings beautiful. In every country associations have been formed for the purpose of encouraging and directing art in the home, and those who are attentive to the moral progress of the masses expect the greatest benefits from this diffusion of simple artistry, joyous and discreet, capable of making a working man love his home more because it is thus rendered radiantly cheerful by art.

Outside of the home, art penetrates that other group which is like an extension of the home, the school. Here is raised the pedagogical question as to the part of art in teaching and in education generally.

No one today doubts the salutary influences exercised by art on the minds of children, of young people. To teach them to love it is to develop the noblest energies, to encourage the purest aspirations of their mental life, to assure them the most exquisite enjoyments in the future. The movement for art in the school is born of these ideas.

The most enthusiastic partisans of art in the school wish to open all the levels of teaching to its beneficent influences. This point of view brings us back to the ideas of the Greeks on integrated education. Did not Plato, in the constitution of his ideal state, require that even the warriors be familiar with music?

The salutary start of this movement should be made in the primary school. It is highly commendable to give to young souls such nourishment, the divine ambrosia that Plato demands for the young men of his ideal republic, on condition that simple beauty is held to and proportioned to the cultural development of the children or of the adolescents. Let there be given to the furniture of the classroom a stamp of good taste perceptible to the unfolding mind; let the students

be addressed on the aesthetics of their school's architecture; let them be shown familiar objects which modern industry has learned to adorn with beauty; let them be made to see the beauties of their locality: the river, the hills, the mountains, the sites in the midst of which they will live and which, without their being trained to do so, they will not learn to admire. Let their attention be drawn to the works of art of their country, the church of their village, the old mill, the historic mansion, and the monuments of the city which they will be able to see. Nothing better. But let not a picture representing the Parthenon or the Temple of Karnak, whose artistic signification is understandable only after long study, be placed before them. It would be a mistake to confuse art with archaeology. The beginnings of aesthetic appreciation must not be archaeological, for archaeology is only a branch of history. Now the history of art, like the history of science or of philosophy, presupposes a manifold knowledge, and is in place only on the higher educational levels. Its place is in the higher schools, in the normal schools, and especially in the universities, where artistic instruction should be the crowning subject of the curriculum.

It is regrettable, in fact, that in the study of the Greek, of the Roman, and of the medieval civilizations all should be encompassed except art, which is the flower of their social life. The plastic art of the ancients is silently passed over in our program, the desiccating German philosophy having killed the aesthetic sense of the masters who were commissioned to explain the Greek and Latin literary masterpieces. Complementary to the instruction, there is also an artistic teaching which rounds out one's education. Man is not complete without artistic culture: Plato, Plotinus, St. Augustine, St. Thomas Aquinas, Dante, Leonardo da Vinci, Leibnitz, Goethe, and Pasteur all had a fine sense of appreciation of the beautiful.

In each of its degrees, the teaching of art in school lends itself excellently to the application of the intuitive method which presents to the pupils artistic models or their reproductions. A person must show the thing he is speaking about. The visual representation gives a teacher the most effective assistance. It is not without interest to note that the triumph of the intuitive method is a splendid confirmation of the principal thesis of Aristotelian and scholastic ideology: that no idea can enter the soul without passing first through the channel of the senses.

Art does not confine itself to the home or to the narrow precincts of the school: it follows man into his public life. It invades the city and the town. Partisans of the art of the street await the innumerable benefits of this other affirmation of its domain: the aesthetics of the city, like architecture and the industrial arts, is inspired with a finality, or end. In days of old, anxiety for security and for defense confined the city within a walled enclosure and furrowed it with narrow passages, each of which could be easily barricaded. The magistrates of the modern city have in view ends of a different sort. They must think of hygiene, of the facilities for traffic and for the surveillance by the police. When we judge of the beauty of the city, we cannot neglect these functions which ought to be evident in the directions of the streets, in the groupings of the buildings, and in all that pertains to the well-ordered arrangement of a collective habitat. But this aesthetic point of view is reinforced by the social point of view: shaded parks, floral patches, boulevards and sidewalks, fountains, public squares ornamented with statues and monuments forming oases where the people can breathe freely, rest, and be revived physically and morally.

The question of the mission of art looms still larger when its social value in the state is considered. As to the moralizing mission of art, the Greek philosophers professed the strange theory that art should not be an indifferent distraction but a social teaching, a lesson for the moral betterment of humanity. They considered themselves authorized by this doctrine to arm the government with the right to regulate every artistic production. Art having, according to them, as its essential *raison d'être* to make men better than they are, they would conclude that it belongs to the government, representing society, to pass judgment as a sovereign master on the moralizing effects of a work of art.

Today we have left far behind the Greek thesis of the right of absolute verdict that Plato claims for the state. To require a government official to be responsible for putting into circulation a work of art would be senseless. But is it necessary to go to the other extreme and formulate the theory that authority should be indifferent toward the artistic production? Highly perfected methods of copying have placed artistic works within reach of the lowliest groups and have made certain applications of them powerful and even formidable vehicles of ideas and sentiments. If these ideas and sentiments were placed at the service of doctrines detrimental to the dignity and security of the citizens; if, for example, art should become inimical to patriotism or still worse should endanger ordinary decency without which human society would become utterly depraved, why could not the state use the repressive rights that all modern legislation concedes to it, and raise an avenging arm to punish the culpable? Is it not on the same grounds that the law is able to prohibit, or at least to regulate, public seances of hypnotism and certain exhibitions of a scientific order? Artists take such interventions ill and carry on lawsuits to attest their general unwillingness to recognize the existence or even the possibility of an artistic misdemeanor. Art indeed would be a sacred thing, and the artist, already relieved of the binding force of conscience, would be, in addition to this, placed beyond the scope of penal laws. A very crude sophism, for it is not art that one condemns in the work, but the social menace which the work propagates. It is attacked, not because of its artistic value, but independently of this value or in spite of it.

The ancients were so strongly imbued with the social role of works of art that they did everything to integrate art with the popular life: the market place, the forum, the temples, and the public baths were adorned with statues, surrounded by colonnades, or covered with decorations. Modern states have been inspired by the same ideas to open museums of painting and sculpture, to acquire historic dwellings, and to encourage legacies of private collections to be made to the state, in order to place works of art within the reach of the general public and to convert them into government property. These have been called museums, buried places of art. It has been said that a work of art removed from the environment for which it was first destined is a work uprooted and stripped of meaning. This saying contains some truth. A museum is not, or should not be, a sort of stock room where the state or the city heaps up its artistic riches. It should be an intelligent exposition, capable of setting forth in relief the individuality of each work and the relationship of the various schools. Some of the great American cities have divided their art collections among different buildings, and certain directors have organized a periodic exodus of certain works, intelligently chosen, to secondary centers in the state. Much progress is yet to be realized in this field.

The collective and national ownership of certain works of art leads us to another question more directly philosophical, which the ideas of democracy and of socialism have put into vogue. It has been repeated again and again that the enjoyment of art, like education, is a universal human right: that art cannot be reserved to a coterie, nor constitute a pleasure merely for the initiated; that it must be put within reach of the rank and file, like the enjoyment of material wealth. Those who, with Herbert Spencer, are satisfied with the mirage of evolution, look forward with enthusiasm to the future of humanity when industrial and mechanial progress will leave to human beings such an abundance of leisure time that everybody will be an artist. While waiting for this dream to become a reality, others wish to popularize artistic enjoyment, to which, they say, the lower classes have the same right as the rich and influential. They admit, of course, that in order to reach such a result art must come from its high pedestal and lower and cheapen itself, for the amount of artistic appreciation which the masses are capable of is very small. "And so it is," said Von Hartmann, "that the theater will be supplied with a kind of vulgar but popular farce, which will amuse the rabble in the public squares."

Nature opposes such pretensions for she creates in individuals such a diversity of imagination, sensibility, or intelligence that the dreamed-of leveling will ever be chimerical. Even though the socialization of every economic means could be arrived at by governmental decree, personalities could never be equalized. By force of circumstances, alongside popular art there will always be a superior art which will remain inaccessible to the crowd. Not that we need to go to the other extreme and demand that art be reserved for a mere coterie and that beauty be enclosed in formulas the sense of which would be grasped by only a handful of the initiate; this would be but to fall into the error that marks every epoch of decadence.

But we hear it said that the understanding of the master-pieces by which humanity is honored, such as Greek statuary, medieval architecture, Renaissance painting, French literature of the seventeenth century, modern music from the time

of Bach, is not easily acquired. We are told that it requires a development of general culture, an education of the faculties perceptive of the beautiful, a grounding in historical, philosophical, and social ideas—in fact, in everything that is the possession of well-endowed natures and the fruit of long and studious efforts.

Finally there arises the last aspect of the civilizing mission of art when it is viewed above and apart from national groups, diverse and multiple, when it is abstracted from time and space and considered a human patrimony of beauty. Are not certain works the collective and permanent possession of all humanity? Yes. Under what circumstances does a work of art become a part of this supranational treasure? When it answers to the eternal aspirations of the human soul, when it speaks a language that man has always understood and will ever be able to understand.

The masterpieces of art escape the deadly clutch of time. The past never makes them grow old. It loads them with memories that render them more precious; centuries pass over them without altering their youth. Thus it is with the great poems of Homer and Virgil which bring to view the virtues and passions anchored in the depths of the human heart. Thus it is with masterpieces of Greek statuary which show in incomparable plastic the chaste beauty of the human body. They respect its nobleness and refuse to tolerate an impure interpretation of its image. Through respect for this body there were created those mythological beings: fauns, tritons, and satyrs to represent human vices. Then again there are the cathedrals of the Middle Ages, those refuges of prayer and enclosures of beauty, the very forms of whose stones cry out to the generations that pass by of the majesty of God dwelling there.

Universal, because it is enriched by the contributions of all peoples; permanent, because it addresses itself to the generations of all times; the treasury of great works of art, like every treasury, is susceptible of indefinite growth. Thus art collecting is, without dispute, one of the highest forms of artistic progress.

This doctrine is not new. It is contained in substance in a splendid letter written by Dante Alighieri to Can Grande della Scala, duke of Verona. Speaking of his *Divine Comedy,* he defines in the following terms the end toward which he worked: "My poem is addressed to all humanity. I wish to draw all the living from the state of misery to a state of felicity." Never has the civilizing and humanizing mission of art been expressed in more concise and eloquent terms.

CHAPTER VIII

Beauty in Nature

ACCESSIBILITY

ALL of us have seen the artist contributing to render resplendent the order he has chosen. Everything in the work of art is intentionally adapted to the capacities of the mental powers of the human beings for whom it is made. There is nothing astonishing about this if the work of art impresses and delights. It is intended to express beauty, and it would not make sense if that were not its definite end and purpose.

Such is not the *raison d'être* of nature. The myriads of electrons, of ions, of atoms, of cells which constitute material bodies are the agents of a drama with its moving scenes arranged according to inexorable laws, which, to borrow the expression of Cournot, "tend fatefully and inevitably toward an end which eludes our vision." No one would dare to flatter himself that he comprehends fully all the purposes of natural processes and phenomena; but it is easy to see that it is not nature's chief finality to appear beautiful to the eyes of human beings. Not that nature is anywhere utterly devoid of beauty. It is beautiful by superaddition of a loveliness which overwhelms our capacities of appreciation. But this beauty is not evident at all times and to everyone. It has need of being understood, of being interpreted, and as this interpretation requires certain conditions of culture it comes not within the reach of every individual. For these reasons beauty of nature is less accessible to the majority of mankind than the beauty of art.

The first hymns of the *Rig-Veda,* which are among the most ancient literary documents of humanity, sing of the power of nature in all its forms; the imagination and the mind of the Hindu poets is impressed by the exuberance of the tropical vegetation; they deify nature, and yet take no notice of its beauty: "In the rudimentary songs of the savage and in all the primitive literatures, in Homer or in the *Chansons de geste,* for example, a plain is hardly ever admired except for its fertility and the richness of its productivity; a man but for his tall stature, his vigor, and his talent." "It is a general fact," continues M. Lalo, "that nature never offers man aesthetic interest by itself outside of artificial ornamentation, and fictitious arrangement of natural growths in the highly civilized epochs." [1] Now, the civilized epochs are those in which the philosophies began to bloom. Certain poets have found

[1] *Revue philosophique,* 1909, p. 499.

it within their hearts to curse nature, as did Alfred de Vigny, who reproaches her for remaining indifferent to our joys and sorrows. Some literary modes have falsified natural sentiments, for example, as when the marquises made themselves shepherds and led the white sheep to pasture with shepherds' crooks trimmed with ribbons. But in a general way one can say that the philosophers have been right in their views of nature, and that they have each inclined, where natural beauty is concerned, to explain it according to the exigencies of their system.

THE HISTORY OF PHILOSOPHY

To convince oneself of this fact one needs but turn the pages of history. Although the Cosmos is the link with the real, a shadow of the Idea, Plato magnifies it and praises its beauty. The *Timaeus* teaches us that in order to ensure the symmetry of the universe, the divine Architect has cleaved the soul of the world through its center and has reunited the two parts in the form of a circle. Very naive and poetical at the same time is the other explanation to which Plato has recourse in order to mark the contents of the world with the imprint of its beauty; the four single bodies (earth, fire, air, and water) are reduced to plane surfaces; and triangles, which constitute the generating forms, are those which realize the proportions most pleasing to the eyes, namely, the right-angle triangle, the isosceles, and the scalene.

In appreciation of the beauty of the sensible world no philosopher of antiquity found expression more effective than

Plotinus, the great representative of neo-Platonism; and when Gnostics frequented his school, he took delight in defending against them the perfections of the universe. The sun, the stars, men, animals, although discarded emanations of the Supreme Being, are nonetheless projections and reflections of His beauty. The ugliness of details is engulfed, he says, in the beauty of the whole "like a dance perfectly executed in the midst of a program of songs and varied music, like a painting in which the painter does not place everywhere colors which are equally beautiful, but gives to each part the color which is fitting to realize the beauty of the whole." [2] Beauty which is measured by being and life, he continues, is identified with light. "That is why the most beautiful body is fire, superior in beauty to all other bodies. It possesses color by its very essence, and this it is which communicates it to others. The body wherein fire does not dominate offers only a faded tint and is no longer beautiful because it does not participate in the whole form of color." [3]

The aesthetic of life and light formulated by Plotinus in his metaphysical principles aroused the enthusiasm of the Alexandrian world, it taught the neo-Platonists and Fathers of the Church, united in the same crusade against the Gnostics, to turn their attention toward the great spectacles of nature. Listen how Denis Longinus, disciple of Porphyry, exalted and magnified the wonders of natural beauty: "Our

[2] *Enneads,* Bk. XXVIII (ed. Kirchoff, 3, 544 A). See J. Cochez "L'Esthétique de Plotin," *Revue néo-schol. de philos.,* 1914.
[3] *Enneads* (Bouillet trans.), I, 103.

admiration does not expend itself naturally on little brooks, though the water be transparent and even useful, but on the Nile, the Danube, and the Rhine, and more than all on the ocean. We are not thrown into wonderment when a little flame which we ourselves have lighted preserves its pure brightness, but we are overcome with awe before the celestial lights, even after they are withdrawn from our vision. Nothing appears more admirable to us in nature than the craters of Etna which spit forth from the bottom of their abysses stones, rocks, and rivers of flame." [4] St. Augustine and St. Chrysostom speak the same forceful language. "Look," exclaims St. Chrysostom, "at the starry heavens, the great plains where the stag and doe freely browse about the fountains, and tell me whether one should not be enraptured by the beauties of nature and by the marvelous works of the Creator."

The aesthetic optimism of the Fathers of the Church was perpetuated by the philosophers of the Middle Ages, but became more coldly rational and dependent, one may say, on a metaphysic of the divine. To meet it in its poetic and living expression one must read the poems of Dante and the *Fioretti* of St. Francis. The Renaissance came, which was foolishly enamored of the beauties of the world; it succumbed to the attraction of natural mysteries; it professed an idolatrous attitude toward nature, making of it a god in order to exalt it above all else. The pantheistic naturalism of Patrizzi and Giordano Bruno surpasses the enthusiasm of the Alexandri-

[4] D. Longin, *Du sublime;* sect. 32, "Difference between Plato and Lysias."

ans, but it does not equal their philosophy in profundity of thought.

Finally, the long series of modern philosophies bursts forth. They fill the last three centuries, and no one of them, it may be said, apart from a few theories of the pessimists, has disregarded the beauties of nature. There is Malebranche who, composing his discourses on metaphysics, revels in admiration of the prodigies with which the world is filled. There is Leibnitz for whom all is for the best in the best of worlds, and who places beauty in a bright obscurity of the psychic life, a confused perception of order. There is Kant who is not less optimistic in his own way and, strange to say, looks for the beauty of nature in the reactions and attitudes of the Ego. There is Rousseau, of whom Jules Lemaître has found it possible to remark that in his solitary eyes are reflected the fields, the woods, the mountains, and the lakes, but to whom there has been attributed unduly the merit of having awakened in the moderns a feeling for nature. We will not continue this enumeration; it would be undertaking a task that leads us away from the plan of our present work.

Ruskin

I cannot conclude this rapid excursion into history without reference to a man who, among our contemporaries, has extolled the beauty of nature in the most vivid prose: John Ruskin. He is in fact the high priest of the religion of beauty. Many of his pages recall the ardors of Plotinus, of Denis Longinus, of St. John Chrysostom. The nature he admires is unviolated nature, away from the environs of the city. He cannot find language sufficiently sarcastic to apply to the modern Sophists who give the name "nature" to "factories, side-walks, hackney-coaches, bicycles, tea-gardens and rail-road enbankments." [5] He loves the deep valleys where the waters, the herbs, the light beams, the shadows, and the dewy moisture turn all to their phantasy.

Nothing translates better the inner thought of Ruskin on the beauty of virgin nature than the cult he professed for the cloud: one of the only things he believed that man could not touch or soil. He would not have hesitated to curse airplanes which now invade the cloud-filled regions. Everything is beautiful which is real, and everything leads to that which Ruskin calls "the signature of God on his work." However great was his love of art, Ruskin was obliged, in order to re-main logical, to place art below nature. "All sound art," he says, "is comprised in a real thing which is *better than art.*" Also, "no Greek goddess has ever been half so beautiful as a young English woman of pure blood." [6] At the end of his life he dreamt of a social philosophy which marked a return to the cult of natural beauty. Since industrialism and specu-lation sacrifice the beauty of the landscape, it would be neces-sary to proscribe both; it would be necessary also to proscribe poverty which in the city destroys the plastic beauty of the body, and to return to a simple life without which the cult of the beautiful is impossible. In the ideal time, which Ruskin

[5] Robert de la Sizerane, *J. Ruskin et la religion de la beauté,* p. 224.
[6] *Ibid.,* pp. 216, 218, 222.

foresaw, no longer would a factory chimney belch smoke into the heavens, and the railroads would be made to sink out of sight into the ground. After this rapid glance at history, let us turn to the study of the beauty of nature.

The Natural Beauty of Nature

An appropriate point of departure is furnished by the teachings of Ruskin, and these will help us to indicate our view of the state of the question, the nature of which is the point under consideration. The nature whose beauty we have set out to study is nature primitive and untrammeled. When the hand of man bends nature to human utilities and its tastes, it can only deform it. The forest "tidied up," the grass cropped, the brook canalized, the tree trimmed and grafted, the flower grown in a green house and watched in its development, may have delightful charm and enter the domain of the ingenious or even of the artistic, but it belongs no more to the domain of the natural, just as the draught horse or the race horse which the trainer has turned from its natural movements, resembles only slightly the wild courser that the Indians used to catch with lassos in the pampas. It will be necessary to choose a special criterion for judging of the beauty or the ugliness of the domestic animal. What is nature? It is the blade of grass with a velvet surface more delicate than the palm of the hand, the reddish brown leaf touched by the sun; it is the mountain, the sea, the plain, and the forest. The United States has set aside as natural reserves vast territories where nature, wild and powerful, with its springs of hot water, its caves, its virgin forests, is protected against aesthetic deformation, and one may well rejoice at the initiation of this movement which other countries are trying to imitate.

These considerations explain why, in order to judge the beauty of nature, we must resist the tendency that inclines us to look always for something human. Nothing is more false that this anthropomorphism, the finding, by way of *Einfühlung,* attributes in animals which belong only to human beings by reason of certain resemblances which they have to man. "In general," writes M. Sully Prudhomme, "an animal appears ugly to us only by our invincible propensity to look for something of the human figure in it." In order to know if there are really ugly monkeys, we would have to consult a monkey, for the beauty that we ask unconsciously in the form of a monkey and that assuredly we do not find there, is human beauty; also, when we say a monkey is ugly, it is as if we said he would be if he were a man; and this is incontestable." [7]

BENEFICENT EFFECTS OF NATURE

A second point presents itself and, thanks to it, there will be removed the illusions of those who imagine that they rejoice in the beauty of nature when they experience only its benefactions. This comes from the fact that those modalities which represent the action of nature on man are complex, and the most powerful ones are strangers to aesthetics.

This is the case with the whole range of organic impres-

[7] *L'Expression dans les beaux-arts,* p. 104.

sions and of the sensible pleasures they engender. Light-hearted friends who, on summer days, organize a picnic or a walk into the refreshing heart of the forest do not, by this fact alone, no matter what they think, become admirers of woodland beauty. They breathe in the oxygen-filled atmosphere and its resinal odors; they revel in the fresh shades and the soothing quiet. Among those who crave the attraction of the mountains, many do not ask anything more than the healthful enjoyment of physical exercise; a bracing contact with the keen air which stimulates the circulation of the blood, a restful contemplation of vast horizons or of the blending colors of the verdure; a walk which reinvigorates the body and engenders wholesome fatigue; climbing and other exercises which make the muscles flexible, flatter self-love, and give a conscious realization of physical well-being.

It is the same with the view of the sea, which more than any other spectacle of nature leads to similar wrong notions. To fill one's lungs with salty sea air is so much more appreciated from the fact that one is escaping the vitiated atmosphere of the cities. The wind in the open stimulates the circulation of the blood, burns the cheeks, tans the skin, while the drafts from the streets or the boulevards often succeed only in making us catch cold. The eye dilates and rests when we let it wander over the even horizon of the water and dunes, and the rhythmical swish of the waves is soothing to the ear. As for air baths, sun baths, and swimming, these give sensations unknown to those who throughout the year live in the close quarters of cities. For all these reasons the sea is the means of supplying health and strength; it rests the body and calms the nerves. Because of the physical benefits afforded there, crowds go to the seashores, causing to arise and to develop those settled regions known as health resorts.

Those who seek nothing else in the forest, at the sea, or in the mountains than the revivifying of vital processes do not enter into communion with the beauties of nature.

We may say as much of another category of lovers of nature, those enamored of her mind-restoring benefits. For she does not only refresh tired organisms; her calm, her silence, the solitude that she affords, and her immensity can renew the soul, relieve mental suffering, and assure momentary forgetfulness of the trials of life. To suffering hearts, the forests and the mountains offer asylums whose soothing influence the poets have sung. Life accumulates deceptions, and the feelings of men change, but nature never changes. The trees are friends that we find from year to year the same, ever faithful. That is one of the reasons why we are surprised that we like them.

Other impressions that nature sustains may be connected with morale building, such as the pleasure of reminiscence. Everyone likes to see his native country, to go over a place where he has sojourned, to revisit familiar sights, because he finds there something of himself, his memories, his loves, his sufferings, a particle of the soul that still clings to the roads over which he has passed. But once again, all that cannot be called aesthetic joy.

Besides the attractiveness that determines their beneficence physical or moral, the lake, the forest, the mountain, all nature furnish inspiration of another order, a love more pure and disinterested: that is the love inspired by their beauty. A new state of consciousness corresponds to it.

The Order Entailed by Nature

Nature is beautiful only on the condition of its being understood. What is requisite to its understanding is a recognition of the order which shines forth from it. Order rules on all levels; it directs the course of the starry heavens as it does the functioning of the microorganisms. The myriads of beings that constitute the material universe are enmeshed in a network of interdependence, the secret of which man will doubtless never guess, as it carries the universe toward an end known to God alone. The thought of Leibnitz remains true: Penetrating eyes like those of God read in a blade of grass the whole history of the world; its present, its past, its future.

When a man perceives some little part of this order, when he recognizes in a being or group of beings the brilliant way nature realizes variety in unity, he rejoices in its aesthetic value. Nature makes herself beautiful for the scholar when he meditates on her, when he interrupts his analyses and researches that he may rejoice in the acquired results. In reference to the phenomenon of cellular division by which nature assures the perpetuation of the species, Rindfleisch writes: "The first time I was witness of it, I asked myself in astonishment: Is it your mind that has been active there? Has the cell the same intelligence as you? If anyone were charged to break in two a long filament such as that . . . would he go about it in a way different from nature's way?" [8] In the same sense we may say with Ruskin that, to relish the real beauty of a rock or of a mountain, we need to be a geologist, "since one part of this beauty resides in the knowledge of the natural laws which have brought on the convulsive earth movements or the slow evolution of the cosmic forces." And when after seventeen years of labor, Kepler discovered the laws that would revolutionize the conceptions of the world, the scholar was silent before the artist and before the adorer, and the beauty of the divine plan drew from his lips a sublime prayer which we cannot read without being moved.

In no place more than on the coast of the Pacific Ocean, in the environs of San Francisco, does a person experience the impression of immensity; yet if he consults only its appearance, the watery plain of Lake Geneva seen from the central parts where no shoreline is visible appears as extensive as the sea viewed from the shores of the Pacific. But as soon as you reason it out, what a difference between the watery expanse which extends to Japan and this inland lake which is only a few leagues in extent! Here we have, from the intellectual side, a proof of the aesthetic properties of nature.

THE SEA

Among the many features making the spectacle of the sea so splendid, some are connected with the magical colors that play on its surface, others with the movements that disturb it,

[8] Rindfleisch, *Aertzliche Philosophie,* 1888, p. 16.

others with the physical force which it obeys. The color of
the water gives pleasure to the eye by the delicacy of its tints,
the gradualness of its transitions, the harmony of its contrasts,
and the perfect blending which our northern seas possess to
so high a degree. It has also an intellectual value, because it
indicates the limits of the different depths, it diversifies
the view, and permits us to perceive the immensity of the
whole. For the marine colors have the power to make the
watery plains stand out, and mark the limits of the various
depths, as in a painting the color accentuates the design and
the perspective. As to movements, who will describe the
variety and unity of the rhythm which agitates these masses
of water, the tide with its pulsations, the enormous wave, or
the gentle ripple which breaks into foam?

Have not the poets since the time of Homer personified
the movement of the sea by attributing human sentiment to
it? We speak of it as calm and sluggish; or we mention its
revolt and its wrath. We regard the ocean as furious when the
western wind shakes it into a tempest. It appears alive because
it is a definitely moving thing, and movement is the outward
sign of life. But we know that the sea does not live, its movement does not belong to the order of vital reality. When we
say the sea is alive, we mean this only symbolically, for we
know there is no reality to the statement.

Upon reflection, we perceive that the sea speaks to the
mind more than to the imagination, and the color and the
movement are only, so to speak, the sensible translation of
this physical force, immense and irresistible, that is the sea.

The mind detects the force of the ocean behind the waves, which ride one over the other; it understands that they obey the winds and the lunar attractions and that, when all has been said, they are an element in the vast concert of cosmic forces. And this force is effulgent, because all that the eye embraces (colors, plans, movements) is multiplied to infinity. Where are we to find language comparable to this? In nature, as in art, the order is beautiful as soon as it is powerfully expressed.

The sea has no need of a frame; it fills all, although the human artist, in order to paint it, is forced to cut off a corner and "to frame it." The shore brings out the immensity of its ordered forces; dunes or rocks give the impression of its resistance to the invasions of the water.

THE FOREST

The order of beauty which impresses in the forest emanates from the abundant life which we see everywhere about. Here we find none of those arranged groves, of those artificial woods where the trees seem to obey a military command and to group themselves at man's direction. Sumptuous vegetation covers vast domains, and the forester confines himself to correcting or directing rank growths, without impeding the exuberance and finality of living nature.

We see that the aesthetic order is revealed differently in the single tree and in the group which forms the forest. The oak speaks in every detail of its robustness; the wrinkled bark, the solid trunk, the wide spread of its heavy boughs, its

rounded top of foliage, the roots exposed to view and so ener-
getically penetrating the soil that they seem "to touch the
realms of the dead." [9] Have you ever noticed how the beauty
of the oak grows when we ponder on its longevity, or when
the sight of an acorn brings us back to its modest origins? It
is then that new relations of order feed the intelligence and
enrich its contemplation. Duration is an indication of
strength, and we understand why the Druids in the forests
of Gaul divinized the tree whose vigor was for them a symbol
of sturdy life.

The seasons in their course display the beauty of the oak
under various aspects, because they put into perspective the
varied manifestations of its vital force. The animating light
of the spring sunshine sets the bark in relief, and warms into
a smile the tender verdure of the leaves. The summer unfolds
the luxuriant and somber foliage. Autumn covers it with
golden spangles and, when December has removed its green
crown, the tree appears all naked, showing the details of its
bony structure. The forms of the leaves and of the branches,
the lines of the trunk and the head, colors of parts and of the
whole, all are ordered and converge toward a unified impression.

What are we to say of the wind, which gives to the tree
the appearance of autonomous movement, and contributes to

[9] In the forest of Bersy, between the Mans and the Château-du-Loir, the Bopp
oak is sixty feet high, as straight as a column. Not a knot mars the trunk which
has developed into a spiral shape; the top is symmetrically developed. This king
tree, surrounded as by a court of other giants, is one of the marvels of the forests
of France.

make of each oak an individuality? The light breeze rustles the leaves without moving the branches; the autumn wind scatters the dying leaves, and again the hurricane's strength shows the power of the gigantic structure. In our northern forests [10] each species of tree has its beauty; the beech tree with its branches slenderer than the oak's and more prolonged, its bark smooth and visible on its trunk, the lush plane tree, the speckled maple; the pitch fir, the larch, the elm, and the birch; all put into play the laws of nature in different ways and reveal to those who understand some of its irreducible relations.

But the forest is clothed with a beauty new and otherwise captivating only when we take in the whole at a glance after considering the individual trees that compose it. The spectator is here ravished with a splendor of order whose richness is inexhaustible, because on all sides appear the strivings for life and its finality.

In the world of vegetation, the struggle for life is the struggle for light, and nature confers the victory on the strongest. What dramas are enacted in the underbrush in the effort of each plant to gain or keep a place in the sun! How skillfully a shrub, hampered in its growth by a powerful neighbor, avoids the latter by growing around it. The oak, lordly master, allows feeble copse-wood to live under its shade; the beech tree, on the contrary, is an egoist that obstructs the light by its tufted foliage. Moreover, we must see how a share in the earth's bounty is contended for where the roots draw in the

[10] The forest of Soignes near Brussels possesses trees of rare beauty.

nourishing moisture, and by what wonders of ingenuity certain plants succeed in solving their problem of procuring food.

Trees die, but the forest lives on. Nature sows the fruitful seeds far and wide to assure the perpetuity of the species. She squanders her means in order to be certain to attain her end. When the crop of acorns is abundant, thousands and thousands of embryonic plants come out of the seeds which the oak has let fall on the ground. Perhaps only one will survive, and it will not be that one which the hand of man would have planted, but the one which the fondling of nature will enable to escape, as by a miracle, from the multiple forces of destruction. The forest forms a vast network of disparate and antagonistic elements whose plan and interaction converge toward an order that is the basis of its beauty. The more we frequent it, the more we realize this.

The woodland takes possession, moreover, of the one who buries himself in its recesses or in its paths, while isolating him and plunging him into a kind of mystery. Let anyone traverse some part of the dense foliage where the shadows and light have full play, let him penetrate the glade where stand a few giants; let him go through it following a slight rise in the ground, from which is abruptly uncovered a panorama of summits, and nature places him face to face with herself.

The Mountain

The forest may become a factor in the aesthetic properties of the mountain. The Ardennes, the Vosges, the Jura, the

Black Forest, the lower Alps, all are wooded regions. In the mountains nature puts to work its most impressive forces, and nowhere is the order which results from their interaction more imposing: the glacier, the moraine, the summits, and the snows give a sensation of pressure and are awe-inspiring applications of the law of gravity. All is struggle and contrast: the torrent leaping over its banks, the cloud rising to scale the mountain, the storm clinging to the slopes of the valley and breaking itself against the masses of stone. The functions of the vegetative life stand revealed in a new light. One senses the force of effort everywhere: in the maple trees whose branches are stripped, in the fir trees which grip the slopes, their roots bestride the rocks in order to find favorable ground; in the Alpine plant, slender, delicate, denticulated, which grows in the depth of a crevice, or on the summit of a crumbling mound, where no one would expect to meet it or would dare to go to pluck it. Summer being short, vegetation is here the more intense, and the flowers are more iridescent, for they gain in brilliance what they lose in duration.

The beauty of nature is, then, distinct from its beneficence. But you will notice that we can enjoy simultaneously or successively the one and the other; and that, on the other hand, we enjoy the beauty less often and for a shorter time. This latter, exacting exercise of the imagination and of the intelligence, is perceived only intermittently, whereas the beneficent effects of the ocean, of the forest, of the mountain act in a continued and permanent way, and surround us entirely.

CHAPTER IX

The Einfühlung

GENESIS OF SUBJECTIVIST CURRENTS

ARTISTIC subjectivism continues to be the vogue. It is the heir of a long past which connects it with the very beginnings of modern aesthetics.

A disciple of Leibnitz, A. Baumgarten, invented the term "aesthetic" and assigned it a special place in the philosophic cycle. It is an explanation of beauty, but in Baumgarten's doctrine, as in that of his master, the beautiful consists in a sensation impervious to order, a clear obscurity of the inner life. It is thus a science of sensation in opposition to logic, which is the science of thought and superior to it.

Thus aesthetics takes its rise in psychology, and since Leibnitz' time there has been the tendency to ascribe it to a certain attitude of the self. The great modern systems have retained from the Leibnitzian doctrine the subjective character of beauty to which every system subscribes, each in its own way. In the course of the nineteenth century, each repudiation of metaphysics retained in its aesthetics an accentuation of the same theory. Accordingly the beauty of art has ceased to be a property of things and has become merely the product of a psychic state.

Kant explains the judgment of beauty in contemplative and sentimental reactions whose secret he looks for, conformably with the general spirit of his criticism, in the very structure of the contemplating mind. This doctrine constituted the basis of German aesthetics in the last century. It inspired the whole German romantic movement and in turn was strengthened by that rapid and brilliant artistic expansion. Schiller, Schelling, and Novalis introduced it into literature, and with Hegel it took on a royal prestige.

In its turn Positivism refused to see in art anything but subjective elements: a free play (Herbert Spencer); a satisfaction agreeable or useful (Guyau).

About the same time, experimental aesthetics, also called "aesthetics from beneath" in a commendable effort based on claims that had to be eventually discounted, applied its method of measurement to representative and emotional states which accompany aesthetic pleasure. Thus it contributed to a strengthening of the conviction that to study the nature of artistic beauty one needs but to analyze what goes on within the subject who enjoys it.

Artistic subjectivism says to us: "To discover the beauty in art, do not go outside your states of consciousness; inclose

yourself within your ego as in an ivory tower." Is it necessary
to obey this injunction? No, it is not. To convince ourselves
of this fact, let us make a rapid survey of a group of aesthetic
theories which have appeared prominently in England and
America, in France and Germany, representing the most
characteristic and most flexible forms of artistic subjectivism.
This survey will help us to understand why a vigorous reaction against it is setting in and why certain excellent minds
wish to open new avenues of investigation in the philosophy
of art.

THE THEORY

It is with a group of German systems we will take up the
discussion first. The hurricane of subjectivism and the
Kantian cyclone that has passed over all the countries of
Europe and America has especially ravaged Germany. It is
from that country that has come the strange form of artistic
subjectivism known under the name of *Einfühlung*, a German term which must be diluted by a paraphrase. Basch and
Lalo, who have worked over it, call it "symbolic sympathy"
and "aesthetic feeling." *Einfühlung* is a projection of our
feelings into the objects surrounding us, a gift of ourselves by
which we pour our very being, all palpitating with sentimental tension and livid emotion, into the being of other things
from which results a sympathetic union between ourselves
and the object. Says Lotze: "We penetrate not only the feelings of life of what is analogous to us in species and essence,
like the joyous flight of a bird or the graceful suppleness of a

gazelle; we penetrate not only the narrow existence of the shellfish to share the pleasure it experiences when opening or closing its valves; we not only expand and spread ourselves with the swaying branches of the tree, but we are capable of conceiving of forms most foreign to ourselves, such as those of an arc or of a regular polygon.[1] This theme developed by Lotze, which has its roots in the most remote German mysticism, has become the leitmotif of a psychological school. The most authoritative representatives of this school are Lipps and Volkelt; and to it have been drawn some English writers, such as Vernon Lee.

The artistic impression, they tell us, is merely a phenomenon of sentimental autoprojection. Let us try, then, to analyze it by applying the French method, the method of clear ideas, which will permit us to separate the chaff of words from the grain of things. In the innumerable examples proposed by Lotze, it seems that the sentimental projection of the self comprises a triple process.

1. A tension or an emotion arises in me when I contemplate an object of art or a being in nature, whether this emotion pre-exists in my soul or appears merely in the wake of the visual contact. At the view of a column I straighten up; with a horizontal line I lie prone; I resist with the keystone which sustains the weight of a pointed arch; I roll over with a circumference. I jump with a rhythmic rondo of Beethoven, just as I languish in a cadence of Chopin; I sadden with the

---

[1] Lotze, *Microcosmos,* Vol. II, trans. Basch, from the citation of Lalo, *Les sentiments esthétiques* (Paris, 1910), p. 77.

cloud, I moan with the wind; I become rigid with the rock, and I smile with the rose.

2. But the impression becomes aesthetic only if it is accompanied by a gift, a loan, an outward sharing of that which is experienced within. I attribute to things what is really my own, and in that way nature lives of my life; works of art become animate, and we both don beauty. In the straight lines and curves, in the geometric forms we transpose, we feel (*Einfühlung*) the forces, struggles, bending, resistance, which really come from us, since they are only modifications of our being, the consequences of the instinct of self-preservation which abides in the very depth of our nature. The rocky crag stands erect and resists through a sort of voluntary tension; to the colors of a canvas we attribute heat and life which belong properly to our own personality; the musical theme contains a spirit of tenderness, of joy, or sorrow like my own; and, in truth, roses smile, clouds lower, winds moan —like human beings. All is humanized and filled with feelings that belong to man alone.

3. The phenomenon is brought to completion in the sympathetic contemplation of this object which has become ourselves and with which we feel ourselves united in the most exquisite communion, so completely that "we no longer are conscious of our loan, but believe that we have become lines, rhythm, sound, cloud, wind, or rock." [2] "Beauty appears," writes Lipps, "when, while contemplating a work, we there

---

[2] Basch, "Les grands courants de l'esthétique allemande contemporaine," *Revue philosophique*, 1912, p. 34.

find, as if in a magnifying mirror, the emotions which constitute the habitual or momentary state of our soul." The
pleasure of art is the complacence we experience on seeing the
reflection of ourselves enlarged and enriched, on reliving in
objects the pulsations of our sentient life.

The German theorists of the aesthetic of sympathy have
pursued in innumerable examples and through the labyrin-
thine analysis of artistic emotions the confirmation of their
ideas. They show that statues become impregnated with
majesty or wrath, with languor or annoyance, according to
the psychic states which dominate the observer and which he
finds expressed in the sculpture. They apply the idea in architecture to the rigidity of the stonework, to the upward sweep
of the pillars, to the push of the vaulted arches, and to the resistance of the flying buttresses, and regard these as functions
which the critic finds in himself and which he lends to the
material objects. Literary work, more precise in the expression
of ideas and sentiments, is of all undertakings the most re-
fractory to this theory; but no art lends itself better than
music to the projection of our inner states outside ourselves.
Rhythm measures our internal movements, melody unfolds
the denouement of our secret dramas; dissonances and con-
sonances, counterpoint and unisons, successions of tones,
these constitute so many feeling values. It is impossible to
imagine a theory which serves more the aesthetic vagaries
of the contemporary polyphonists. When we follow Lipps
in his remarks on the subject of musical sounds, we naturally
think of the ambitions of a Wagner or a Strauss. The theory

of *Einfühlung* contributes to perpetuate the false aesthetic which reduces all musical beauty to the production of a state of sensibility. In one of Chopin's waltzes, executed or heard under an impression of melancholy or sadness, you will believe you discern complaints and cries of despair; and perhaps the melodic chant with its ternary rhythm, its accentuated balance, will incite you to an outpouring of tears, real tears, gushing from the depth of your being and bringing the relief which is so soothing to those who are able to cry. Sorrow expressed; sorrow assuaged. Play or listen to the same waltz at other times, in hours of joyousness or hope, and you will find there, if you wish, an expression of altogether different sentiments.[3]

CRITICISM

But this example launches us into the realm of criticism, and objections crowd upon our minds, so numerous and so imperious that they give the effect of strangling the theory in a bewildering network. And then, in such a conception, what becomes of the technique of the work of art, such as the working out of a poem, the modeling of a statue, the coloring and drawing of a picture, the composing and interweaving of a symphony? All that must count for very little. It is nothing more than soot left from the flame. The perception of forms, of symmetry, of coordination, is only a preliminary and no longer the constituent of the aesthetic

[3] The sentiment which affects us when we are on the point of making certain decisions influences us no less in our practical judgments. "Prout unus quisque affectus est, ita judicat."

impression; the work reputed to be perfect in form is beautiful only in the measure that one's personality pours out the moving and palpitating mass of its own feelings. Therefore, if I can find my sentiment of melancholy or joy in one of Chopin's waltzes, I can also find it in an imitation made from commonplace premises and deprived of artistic inspirations, just as I can deposit my jewels in a cheap casket or in a fine silver cup chiseled by Cellini. In matters of sculpture and painting, the theory obliges us to attribute the same value to copies as to originals. The sentiment which I lend to Mona Lisa with her sly, disdainful smile, with her large eyes, which scrutinize the depth of my soul, I discover, not only in the authentic painting which has gained a place in the *Salon Carré* of the Louvre, but also in the innumerable reproductions which have popularized the enigmatic physiognomy. And we can say as much of the intricate work in plaster or in electrometallurgy to which the progress of industry has given so wide a distribution. If it were thus, technique would become a valueless accessory of beauty, and acceptance of the theory would amount to pronouncing the death sentence on artistic effort.

From such inadmissable deductions we are able to put our finger on the falsity of the theory of the *Einfühlung*. This phenomenon of sentimental autoprojection is not the aesthetic phenomenon. It is only one of the multiple circumstances which accompany a properly artistic impression. That which confirms this observation and furnishes at the same time a second argument against the sympathetic aestheticism is that autoprojection does not always accompany artistic pleasure; its existence is not a universal phenomenon. A figure of Bach may unroll to our charmed ears its themes and its voices, its rhythms and its nuances, without ever surprising us into inserting its sonorous weaving into any episodes of our emotional life. "There is no place here for sentiment, and one must guard against admitting it." [4] It delights the musician by its technical qualities, the purity and elegance of its melodic lines, the marvelous composition of its detail, and the impeccable unity of the whole.

"In addition to this," rightly remarks Lalo, "when it is question of a work of art of multiple elements, how is one to conceive the sentimental projection of the audience into the work contemplated? Such an operation is practically impossible in the scene of a drama where several personages of varied degrees of intelligence, of opposite sexes, and of different temperaments mingle in conversation." [5]

All that has just been said brings to light the fundamental error of the aesthetic of sympathy: it reduces the beauty of art to a purely subjective phenomenon, to the most capricious and most variable of our states of consciousness: feelings. It envisions artistic beauty as no longer possessing any per-

[4] André Pirro, *L'Esthétique de Jean Sébastien Bach* (Paris, 1907), Introduction, p. 3. And he continues: "Here it is only a matter of well-regulated and carefully proportioned figures which it would be extremely ridiculous to judge according to a whimsical and poorly trained sensibility all too ready to become excited. A sound criticism and a high degree of prudence are needed to avoid falling into serious error in the delicate task of determining the value and the meaning of musical works."

[5] Charles Lalo, *Les sentiments esthétiques,* p. 78.

manence; it is not stable. It will be beautiful in different ways according to the sentimental powers of those who contemplate it. For the same man the beautiful will be altogether different tomorrow from what it is today or what it was yesterday, since it follows that wavelike ebb and flow of the affective life. More than that, one will have to say that on certain days the best of masterpieces are devoid of beauty; and this for the reason that I have neither the desire, the need, nor the courage to lend them my soul. This is subjectivism and relativism: a subjectivism much more complete than that of Kant, who at least attributed to the judgment of beauty a character of universality, the release of contemplative functions obeyed by all men in uniform laws. Artistic subjectivism leads to abysses which we shall discuss at length after passing in review other forms of the philosophy of art prevalent in France, in America, and in England, which also attempt to enclose artistic beauty in the internal forum of one's consciousness.

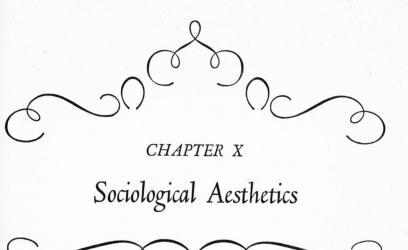

CHAPTER X

Sociological Aesthetics

THE THEORY

SOCIOLOGICAL aesthetics, brilliantly defended by a group of French writers, is a branch of the contemporary sociological school whose tendency is to see only social values in human facts. The sociologists are far from agreeing on the object of sociology, and the Academy of Moral Sciences in Paris was well inspired when it offered a reward to anyone who would fix the exact and reasoned limits of this young and seductive science, with its undetermined contours.[1] Some few of its promoters are willing to assign to it as a field of study certain collective phenomena and their interactions. But others include in its domain the states of individual consciousness, and especially the judgments that we pass on the morality of conduct and on the beauty of works of art. Thus

[1] I do not know whether the prize was ever awarded.

if we say: "The soldier who serves his country accomplishes a sacred duty," or "The landscapes of Corot are admirable," these judgments would have no other value than mere reflections on collective life. In a series of recent publications, Charles Lalo expounded and defended this new form of the philosophy of art. It constitutes the pendant of the moral sociology of Durkheim, so highly regarded in France, and the analogies are such that the two theories resemble the two tablets of a diptych. I propose to define and criticize the ideas that inspire this philosophy and to clarify the study by showing its relation to sociological morality.[2]

The judgment of morality and the judgment of artistic beauty are social values. What does this mean? The idea of value is linked to the idea of the utility which accrues from a thing to the person possessing it. Some values appeal to only one person or several persons; others are considered such by a multitude more or less numerous. The familiar objects, which the pious hand of an ambulance driver gathers from the pocket of soldiers dead on the field of battle, are precious souvenirs for parents and friends, but objects of indifference to those who are strangers to the family. The flag, on the contrary, has a collective and socialized value. In the defense of the flag the soldier sacrifices his life, and all of us uncover our heads before the glorious emblem of our country. Now the beauty of a work of art is of a social and not of an individual value: such is the starting point of Lalo's

[2] Applying the same directive to the study of religious beliefs, Protestant writers have sought the criterion of their truth in the variable assents of groups.

thesis. That means to say that a work of art is beautiful only if it is recognized and in the measure to which it is recognized by a group, by a public. A writer, says Lalo, who would be the only one enamored of his work and who would, in his own unsocial isolation, believe that his work was not to be admired by others but by himself alone, would enjoy personal satisfaction, but this satisfaction would have "no right to be called aesthetic so long as it remained strictly individual." [3] "There is no art without value," he concludes, "as in fact, there is no value which is not social."

What confers on a work of art a social character and therefore its value, is the obligation, the force, the pressure, the authority, which derives from the social organization, and thanks to which its beauty imposes itself on the group. Therefore, if you wish to know if a work of art is beautiful, question its contemporaries, take the advice of the generation in which the work has sprung up: the approval or the disapproval of the group is the criterion of beauty. The literary circles at the time of Augustus admired the talent of Virgil; the pontifical court of Julius II paid homage to the genius of Michelangelo; as today, the public has an appreciation for the paintings of Corot. The works of Virgil, of Michelangelo, of Corot are beautiful by virtue of this approbation, of this judgment of the public that approves and applauds it. Thence this second formula of Lalo: "The aesthetic value is glory and admiration." [4] Now you can understand why the satisfaction of

[3] *Revue philosophique,* July, 1914, p. 47.
[4] *Ibid.*

a solitary or a maniac, who jealously reserves to himself the monopoly of a painting, of a sculpture, of a poem, or of a symphony would be only the outer fringe of the enjoyment of art; apparently this man could not concede to himself the glory without which the work has no beauty. "All art presupposes a public, the sovereign distributor of aesthetic sanctions." [5] If this is so, then the public does not contribute the glory and the success because the work of art is beautiful; but the work is beautiful because the public applauds it. One may see that with such principles the philosophy of art becomes a science of pure observation and inquiry into the conditions which determine collective evaluations, and into the genesis and variations of the public's approving attitude.

At this point the philosophy of art is linked with social morality, which its partisans reduce to a science of morals based on experience. For them morality of human acts is but another kind of social value, and it is socialized by the same procedures as confer beauty on works of art. An action is good or bad according to the judgment emanating from a collective consciousness, deciding whether this particular action is good or bad. Do you wish to know whether the killing of deformed children, or the putting to death of important old men is an action morally good or bad? Consult the consciences of social groups: the Spartans considered these homi-

[5] Lalo, *Les sentiments esthétiques,* p. 206. "All art presupposes a public, the sovereign distributor of aesthetic sanctions: a public present or future, real or even imagined as simply possible, universal or restricted to a milieu popular or selected. Even King Louis of Bavaria, when he indulged the insane luxury of having presented before himself alone a Wagnerian drama, must have created for himself, in his insane mind, the mentality of an audience."

cides a measure of wisdom, conforming to their ideal. At the time of the unsocial Greek city, these actions were normal; therefore, moral. Today they are repugnant, and the collective judgment of civilized social groups would brand as murderers the instigators of such monstrous practices.

But, then, you will say: Has what was moral twenty centuries ago become immoral today? Is what was beautiful at the time of the Greeks no longer beautiful today. Perfectly. The norm which a collectivity attributes to itself to decide the morality of human actions and the beauty of human production, is a norm that varies with the societies of which it is only a product; we call it the ideal for the conduct of man and we call it technique for the works of art. According to Durkheim, society has a soul which develops collective forces superior to individual forces. It creates its ideal in periods of effervescence and great crisis: the establishment of Christianity, the rush of men of intellect to the University of Paris during the Middle Ages, the humanism of the sixteenth century, the revolution of 1789, and the socialism of the nineteenth century were born during these moments of feverish exaltation. But these are transient states owing to their very violence. Hence the need of nourishing the cult of the ideal by holidays, by orations, by reunions, by manifestations of all kinds which assure the periodic renaissance of the creative crisis. The ideal evolves with society. It is the same with artistic technique. It undergoes the fluctuations of the collective consciousness which gives rise to them. The aesthetic conscience—the word comes from Lalo—creates a law of beauty from its tendencies and tastes; and consent of a notable group creates the social commandments.

The contemporaries of Phidias required the sculptor to place the accent on the symmetry and the plastic regularity of the human body. Even the most violent muscular movements must not violate the grace of the form, as one can see by considering groups of wrestlers and discus throwers. These works are beautiful because they obey the social injunctions of the time. The Athenian public would have pitilessly condemned the diversified art of a Constantine Meunier, whose types of miner, of river-porters, and of harvesters at work arouse the admiration of our contemporaries. The collective approbation in matters of art, as in matters of morals, rules the attitude which we assume when face to face with works of art, and it is this which Lalo calls the normative side of aesthetics. For the approbation of a group, more or less notable, has its sanctions that a person must not defy, any more than he can set aside with impunity the habits of good breeding and the moral ideas of his time. "The aesthetic conscience has its satisfactions and its remorses, its austerities and relaxations, its revolts and its capitulation, its refined decencies and its cheap buffooneries, its positive and negative sanctions: glory, and admiration or failure, and ridicule." [6] Social sanctions being everything, it is not astonishing if what is beautiful today was not so yesterday and will not be tomorrow; if every form of new art appears arbitrary because it disturbs popular habit, and if all forms of

[6] P. 258.

ancient art are treated by the rising generation as an out-
moded garment.

We are presented with the conclusion that the concrete
and normal aesthetic fact "is respect for established technique and disdain of all that deviates from it. Innovations
are not beautiful; they become beautiful; before imposing
themselves as an ideal they are judged hideous by everyone
except the author." [7] If innovations are never beautiful because they clash with the existing techniques, if on the other
hand they become beautiful on the day when they are imposed, artistic beauty is nothing stable, nothing immutable;
it is carried along by pure relativism. Lalo recognized this
fact. "Relativism means that there is nothing absolute, that
everything is relative to everything else, that our opinions
are relative to those which preceded and to those of other
men with whom we form a solid social group into which our
individuality enters and which reacts on us." [8] The principle
of this chronic decline of the aesthetic ideal was consequent
upon the periodic decline of the moral ideal.

CRITICISM

After this exposition of sociological aesthetics, let us consider its insufficiencies and the labyrinth of difficulties into
which it draws us.

Let us ponder for a moment on what would become of our
aesthetic judgments if it were true that the work of art has

[7] P. 207.
[8] Pp. 207 f.

meaning only as social consecration and that it is subject
to disappear on the day when admiration for it will come "to
be socialized"; that is, when a new form will be sanctioned,
and, following the happy expression of Arreat, its value is
subject to ups and downs like those on the stock market.

If it were thus, the works of art of the past would have
only an archaeological and retrospective interest; one would
make a collection of them as memorials of human culture as
one does with vehicles, or musical instruments which have
served their day; but they would be stripped for us of attraction and of aesthetic significance. How would the existing
generation be inspired with the beauty of the temples of
Karnak, with the statues of Phidias, with the paintings of
Leonardo da Vinci, now that formulas of art, which are socialized today by the taste of the public, have rendered unfash-
ionable for centuries the works that were assured of glory in
the Thebes of Rameses II, in the Athens of Pericles, or in the
Florence of the Medici?

Nothing is more untenable. Homer, Dante, Molière, La
Fontaine, Racine, Corneille, Beethoven, Shakespeare are of
all time; they will continue to command the admiration of
passing generations because of the indelible imprint of genius
by which their works are marked. Humanity makes no mistakes there; underneath the changing garments which circumstances proper to each epoch impose on the masterpieces,
it recognizes the unchanged character of beauty.

It is not otherwise than with the idea of justice, of virtue,
of honor, and of all these things of nobleness which form

the prerogatives of the human species. The great voice of the moral conscience rises likewise across the centuries, and dominates the maelstrom of societies which are born and disappear. Even though they clothe themselves in variable modalities from one moment of history to another, even though pride, passion, the ambition of a certain social coterie, or the psychological climate might well veil them, obscure them, the precepts of the natural law impose themselves unchanged on the consciences of all men who appear in successive generations here on earth. Moral heroism and artistic beauty have eternal youth. The spirit hails and cherishes them wherever it meets them.

But Mr. Lalo has foreseen the objection that arises when one considers the enthusiasm our contemporaries have for the artistic forms of the past, the interest which the exhibitions of the art of bygone ages arouse and of all that points to value in the ancient techniques. He attributes this enthusiasm to an illusion. "We have seen that a natural illusion makes us attribute a constant and absolute value to what has in reality only a variable one, and that more or less personal. Therefore all that we admire of the techniques of the past seem to us to have always had, even at the time when they lived, the same and immutable value that we ascribe to them today and they can offer no other. We live in a period which in certain respects and for certain arts is undoubtedly an age of decadence, like most decadences it is extremely eclectic, in part by reason of legitimate love of history, in part because of a regrettable lack of outstanding personalities and of strongly marked tastes. Thus, then, when we appreciate highly, side by side and under the same title, the Gothic furniture and a salon of Louis XV, a French garden and an English or Chinese park, a Gregorian gradual, a polyphonic motet, an aria of an opera, and adagio of a symphony, a Hindu pagoda, a Greek temple, a Gothic cathedral, a Renaissance palace beside our modern-styled homes, we do not sufficiently reflect that the taste of each one of the generations which have made these diverse forms of art live was much more pronounced and restrictive than our own." [9]

But no, we are not dupes when we admire the ancient masterpieces; the analysis of our intimate feelings protests against this explanation. Not only in the epoch of decadence, if it so happens that we live in an epoch of artistic decadence, but in the ages of splendor, there has been paid a unanimous veneration to the great works of the past. Did not the sculptors of the Renaissance place themselves in the school of the ancients? Certainly the study of vanished civilization intensifies the artistic impression aroused by the works from which they were born, for that impression penetrates every detail beneath and around the works. It is true to say that archaeology well understood serves the cause of art.[10] But it is not necessary to be a scholar and an archaeologist in order to be swayed by the charm of a masterpiece of antiquity or of the Middle Ages. Anyone can appreciate them without books,

[9] Pp. 234 f.
[10] See above, chap. 6.

without culture, without witnesses, without a guide, provided he has something of the artistic temperament.

More than that, works like Homer's *Iliad,* the *Venus de Milo,* Molière's *L'Avare,* the fables of La Fontaine, and many others are nearer to us because more profoundly and intensely human than these "futurist or cubist" productions for which certain critics carve a niche of glory. Is it not incontestable that some epochs had false tastes, and that the history of art has known some inferior techniques, decadent styles which, however, in their time were denied neither praise nor popular acclaim? Let it suffice to cite the allegorical romances of the Middle Ages, the childish verses of Jean Antoine de Baif which letters patent of 1570 approved in an *Academie de Poesie et de Musique;* [11] or again the literature of the *Précieuses* at the hotel de Rambouillet.

I admit that in Lalo's theory each of these techniques had its hour of beauty, and was calculated to last as long as the mode to which it submitted. But I no longer understand by what right the artists, the historians of art, and the critics, who live and write today, venture to condemn certain techniques or establish a gradation among dead techniques, which by definition should have an equal value. If we are justified not to put on the same plane of beauty Chapelain's *Pucelle* and Racine's *L'Athalie,* it is because we make use of a norm, of a criterion, which is not the success which they both enjoyed in their respective environments. Should not every

[11] Brunetière, *Histoire de la littérature française,* I, 406.

artistic innovator swim against the current and brave the tyranny of the prevalent fashion? And when the fashion is bad, is it not the artist who is right when he sets himself against it? Boileau did well to denounce the bad taste in literature which prevailed in the salons of the seventeenth century and to prefer to it the art of Corneille, Molière, and Racine. The beauty of the great classics is not, therefore, comparable to a financial value which falls or rises according as it loses or recovers the favor of the capitalists.

Indeed success may be an index of the value of art, but success does not constitute that value. And the same index is far from being infallible. "Was the work of Wagner," observes Arreat, "any less valuable when it was hissed in Paris and is it more valuable now when it is acclaimed? Further, would the value depend upon the number of singers employed or upon the quality of their voices? If it is the number that rules, to what extremes this strange use of universal suffrage would lead! And if it is the quality, then will not one voice suffice to establish its value and merit?" [12]

When Lalo, the chief theorist of sociological aesthetics, reproaches the German sentimentalist upholders of *Einfühlung* for not weighing the technical value of art, he forgets that this criticism turns against his own doctrine, for he also looks for the beauty of art in the mind of the spectator or listener. What is, in fact, this approbation, a state of soul occurring simultaneously in a large number of individual

[12] Arréat, *"Valeurs d'art. L'Esthétique sociologique,"* Revue philosophique, March, 1914, p. 274.

minds? In such a theory, approbation alone is important; the technique has no aesthetic significance. Let us close here the discussion of sociological aesthetics: we will consider shortly which portions should be retained, and those for which a correction must be found.

CHAPTER XI

Humanist or Pragmatist Aesthetics

PRAGMATISM

PRAGMATISM undertakes to reform the theory of judg-ments, to plunge them into the "continuous stream of consciousness," to make them take root in the real needs of life and thus to give them a more human meaning. From this arises the name of humanism that has been given to the theory. A judgment is true or false according to the purpose it serves, an interest of relevance to someone. Mr. Schiller, a professor at Oxford, writes: "I stroll through a forest with-out a desire to arrive at any special place, and here a cross-road opens before me. Which is the right road? There is none. There will not be a right road for me, and an error in my choice will become possible only if I have the intention to go to a determined place, to the north, for example. From this moment I will be on the right road, or I will take a false route according as I will proceed toward my goal, or thread a by-path which will lead me astray. The *correct* road is the *good* road. Thus it is with science. To decide the *quality* of a scientific judgment observe it when it is being used. Adjustment which leads to good effects is accepted as true while that which leads to unacceptable conclusions is false." Relevance expresses a relation with utility to the one who gives a judgment, but this revelance becomes effectively true only if it gives satisfaction to a social state.

Hence, says Schiller, it follows that "the truths of a generation become the errors of the following generation when the latter has created ways more valuable and more efficacious for interpreting and manipulating the apparent facts which the new truths constantly transform. Inversely, that which is now designated error may engender a large progeny of truth." [1] What becomes of artistic beauty in such a philosophy? This is easy to see. If humanism or pragmatism does not hesitate to divest scientific judgments of stable character in order to make rules of action variable according to time and location, it will find no difficulty in admitting that the artistic works which cease to please cease to be beautiful.

You can recognize immediately a new shoot from the old stump of artistic subjectivism and relativism, and you already foresee the points of contact which will arise between the aesthetics of *Einfühlung* and sociological aesthetics on the

[1] *Error.* A lecture given in 1910 to the International Congress of Philosophy at Bologna.

one hand, and pragmatist aesthetics on the other. The perception of art will participate in all the fluctuations of the judgments of truth. For William James will tell us that the perception of art is but a judgment of truth about a canvas, a statue, a monument, a symphony with, in addition, an emotional shock, a delicate tremor. "In every art," he writes, "in every science, there is a keen perception of certain relations being right or not, and there is the emotional flush and thrill consequent thereupon. And these are two things, not one. In the former of them it is that the experts and masters are at home. The latter accompaniments are bodily commotions that hardly feel, but that may be experienced in their fullness by cretins and philistines in whom the critical judgment exists at its lowest ebb." [2] Thus, what James calls the tremor of art, the emotional shock, which he compares to a vibration of the keyboard of harmony which is our body, presupposes a judgment about the truth of the work of art, and this truth of the pragmatic order is a function of the interest which it is susceptible of engendering. "Nothing shocks me." "Such," reports James, "was the high praise Chopin gave to a musical composition which appealed to him as beautiful"; [3] and it is probable that Chopin would not have used this language upon hearing the works of Claude Debussy. Hence the work of art ceases to be beautiful when it ceases to excite our interest or to be suited to our reactions; it no longer falls then in the field of application of our prag-

[2] *Principles of Psychology,* chap. 25, p. 472.
[3] P. 101.

matic choice; we must go in search of new beauties to experience the use of other productions. The beauty of a work of art resembles an ephemeral drop of dew, which the rays of the sun cause to sparkle like a diamond and then devour. Pérès, in his study of pragmatic aestheticism published in 1911 by the *Revue philosophique,* finds that this philosophy of art accommodates itself marvelously to the artistic productions of our contemporary schools. I think, on my part, that aesthetic pragmatism succumbs completely under its own contradictions and its inadmissible consequences.

This is not the place to play the prosecuting attorney to humanism and pragmatism. It is a strange way this, to build up knowledge by repudiating the principle of the immutability of laws. If our experimental science would have to change with every need of new activity, all prevision of the future would be illusory. Henry Poincaré opposes the pretentions of certain pragmatists with a statement that stuns like the blow of a club: "Knowledge will be either intellectual, or it will not exist at all." Logic would require the pragmatist to admit the mutability of judgments, even when there is question of the directing principles of all knowledge, even of those "judgments of right reason" which Aristotle and Leibnitz rightly declared independent of the existence of a real world. Some pragmatists like Roustan, whose manual is followed in certain schools of France, does not hesitate to explain the formation of these principles by successive gropings to which our ancestors devoted themselves, by a progressive elimination of other recognized sterile formulas, and finally, by the hereditary transmission of the assemblage of approximate judgments, true enough for the needs of life and for the control of nature.[4] There has been a remote epoch, we are told, very remote, when man had not yet found these "first uniformities" (W. James), not even the useful formula which assures us that 1 is not 2, and 2 plus 2 equals 4. I should like someone to show me in the numerous documents pertaining to the youth of humanity the vestiges of these extraordinary adaptations. Should not the bookkeeping of the Pharoahs, for example, which brings us to times passably remote, reveal some deflection from the elementary truths of arithmetic? There is nothing of that. As long as the pragmatists cannot be supported by facts attesting evident variations of the direct principles of knowledge, one will be justified in opposing to them the dictum of Aristotle: "He who presumes to deny the perpetuity and universality of the principle of contradiction is not a man but a blockhead." We hold here that there are some speculative immutable truths, just as there are artistic beauties which will remain so as long as humanity lasts.

This theory of pragmatist aesthetics is set forth in contemporary works through the critique of principles which we have just sketched. Nothing is more personal and more subjective than the interest which dictates judgments of beauty, and with that as a basis there unwinds a chain of inadmissable consequences, of false interpretations that we have already set forth and cannot develop further without

[4] Roustan, *Leçons de philosophie, Psychologie*, p. 421.

repeating ourselves. You see clearly that, in fact, the pragmatists tend to build the beauty of art on the moving sands
of the fleeting impression, on the changing reaction. Technique has no value; it is at the utmost, says W. James, an
"ingredient which excites us." [5] This is artistic subjectivism.
At the same doctrinal crossroads we meet the philosophy of
Einfühlung, the sociological aesthetics, and the aesthetics of
pragmatism. All three have for the last word: "It is not the
works which are beautiful; it is rather our states of consciousness, whether we lend them to the objective (*Einfühlung*),
or harmonize them with the tastes and the commandments
of the collective consciousness (aesthetic of sociology); or
whether, finally, we live them as interesting reactions (the
aesthetic of pragmatism).

THE AESTHETICS OF THE VITAL SENTIMENT

It would be easy to enlarge upon this inquiry into artistic
subjectivism. While passing over a large category of writers,
like Tolstoi and Josephine Peladan, who are artists, but poor
art critics and pitiable philosophers, we could easily find
psychologists whose doctrines deserve to be recalled. One of
the best known in France, M. Guyau, combined the point of
view of *Einfühlung* with that of sociological art in the vindi-
cation of the vital sentiment. [6] He writes: "To appreciate a
landscape it is necessary to be in harmony with it. To understand the rays of the sun we must vibrate with them; we

---

[5] *Op. cit.,* p. 470.
[6] *L'Art au point de vue sociologique,* p. 14.

must tremble with the golden stars, and, to understand dark-
ness, we must feel the chill of the shadowed spaces of vague
and unknown immensity. To enter into the joy of spring we
must have in our heart something of the lightness of the but-
terfly's wing, whose fine dust we breathe from the spring
air." A few lines farther on: "If the feeling for nature is already a social feeling, for a stronger reason all the aesthetic
sentiments excited by our similar ideas will have the character
of sociability. As the sentiment of beauty is raised to a higher
plane, it becomes more and more impersonal."

CONCLUSION

It would retard us uselessly to try to follow the meanderings of the philosophy of Guyau and that of other isolated
writers. The study that we have made of the three great cur-
rents of the philosophy of art has made us recognize well
enough more general tendencies of contemporary subjectivism. From this study we may conclude: Excessive subjectivism does not give an account of the entirety of the aesthetic
fact.

Without denying any of the elements of the impression
felt by the subject, it is necessary to turn to the side of the
object, that is, to the work of art, in order to discern there the
objective factors intimately correlated with this impression.
It were wise to look for the aesthetic phenomenon in the correspondence of one to the other; and, by way of consequence,
to restore to the masterpieces the objective qualities which
inhere in them, and which, by their permanence and their

depth, explain the esteem they have enjoyed through the centuries. Not any more than the heritage of scientific truth or that of moral principle does the heritage of artistic beauty give itself over periodically to conformity with the merely new. Established and enriched during the course of the centuries by way of slow deposits, it has been transmitted from generation to generation. It is the collective good of men, and its conservation and aggrandizement are confined neither to the individual nor to nations, but to the great human family.

CHAPTER XII

Return to Objectivism

Its Manifestation in All Domains

At the present time we have evidence of a new contemporary philosophy. There is a sort of return to metaphysics; an admission that general ideas and principles give us some glimpses of extramental reality. On all sides there is manisfestation of this renewal of objectivism. The theories of art will experience a trend in new directions.

When it is a question of science, see how well the problem of certitude is solved in its more practical doctrines; note too the growing popularity of realism, which recognizes in human knowledge a right understanding of the extramental world. Intellectualism is on the way to execute a brilliant retaliation on pragmatism, the philosophy of action. It holds its head victoriously above the pretensions of scientific relativism. Now here, now there, in England and America, as well as in France, objectivism is being reborn like the phoenix rising from its ashes.

Again, consider the about-face of the contemporary spirit —the word is Paul Bourget's—in the matter of morals, and the large number of excellent minds that recognize the necessity of submitting the principles of private and public conduct to a system of stable norms. The great truths by which the consciences of people survive are being stripped of all the crassness of sophism and are appearing in the greatest clearness.

At the same time the philosophy of art is being newly clarified, and various indications show that a return to objectivism is on the eve of being accomplished. Voices rise up in France and in Germany to react against tyrannical psychologism and to put back in its place the objective factor. Max Dessoir, who organized the last International Congress of Aesthetics in Vienna, proclaims the dependence on the objective where the artistic sentiment finds itself face to face with the beautiful thing. "We must take account of the aesthetic reality," he writes. "It must be established before all else that the laws immanent in the experience of the beautiful cannot be reduced simply to psychological laws and that artistic truth is not identified with psychological truth." [1] In the same way M. L. Arreat protests in the *Revue Philosophique* against the abuses of sociological aestheticism.[2] Doing justice to the changing approbation of the public and the

[1] *Zeitschrift für Aesthetik und allgemeine Kunstwissenchaft,* V (1910), 99.
[2] March, 1914.

enthusiasm of the masses, he shows with clearness how im-
potent are the doctrines which insist in principle on the
instability of artistic norms, and he proclaims the need of
"replacing the value of art in the work itself." In pages too
few in number which he has devoted to the aesthetic experience, Bergson points out the role of the work and of the idea
which it suggests to us. He assigns an enormous influence to
the beautiful object itself since its purpose is "to put to sleep
the active or resisting powers of our personality," to such an
extent that in poetry "our soul, rocked and soothed, forgets
itself as in a dream to think and see with the poet." [3] We can
but applaud these words. It is not the object which fills itself
with the feelings of the subject, but rather inversely, it is the
subject, the ego, which subjects itself docilely to what the
artistic object expresses.

The Objectivity of Artistic Beauty

But we may go still further and discover direct proofs of
the objectivity of the beautiful. The investigation is worth
the trouble, for we must not be satisfied with showing the
harm of subjectivism in order to establish the truth of artistic
objectivism. The discussions on the subject of certitude which
this question again raises as a particular application, have
taken on a considerable enlargement, and interest in them
shows no signs of diminishing.

To those who are not familiar with subtleties of contemporary philosophy, it may seem strange that we must demon-

[3] *Données immédiates de la conscience*, p. 11.

strate the intervention of the causality of the work of art in the production of the aesthetic effect. One may ask: "Are not the cathedral of Chartres, the paintings of Claude Lorrain, beautiful in themselves, and of themselves?" "No," the relativists would exclaim. "To believe so would be to allow oneself to be taken in by the mirage of naive realism.

That it is not a question of mirage can be proved by introspection. We can see ourselves impressed by the work of art. We realize that we are passive in viewing the cathedral even before we assume the artist's attitude; using the exact words of the psychologist, we receive an artistic shock. Now the shock does not come from oneself; it is therefore a non-ego which holds us under its influence, an object distinct from ourselves, a monument or statue, painting or symphony, drama or poem, whose technique stimulates in us the whole gamut of emotions so meticulously investigated by contemporary psychologists. Reality holds us in its grasp; its action is enveloping and tenacious.

If anyone is still tempted to doubt this truth, let him ponder the well-considered pronouncements of competent judges on the value of artistic productions. Where will the motif be found which determines the value if not in the work itself and in the elements of its composition? It is beyond question, then, that these latter have the power to act on the connoisseur. Would you doubt this when the artists themselves yield to the influence of their work after having created it? Is this not the case in the myth of Pygmalion, the king of Cyprus, who fell in love with the statue of Galatea sculptured with his own hands? And did not Michelangelo call out to the marble of his Moses: "Now come alive!"

Let us conclude. The contemporary forms of artistic subjectivism exaggerate the role of the impression of art. Each one of them contains a kernel of truth. To the partisans of the aesthetics called *Einfühlung,* we will say: "The phenomenon of the sentimental projection is real, but it is adventitious and does not constitute the entire aesthetic experience." To the sociologist: "The impression of art is dependent on the environment in which the work comes to fruition." To the pragmatists: "It rests on an interest, on a vital reaction whose nature we have explained." But each of these systems sins by exclusiveness because it denies the aesthetic function of the work of art itself. To meet beauty on the way, we must take into consideration both the impression and the work of art which inspires it.

CHAPTER XIII

The Aesthetics of the Thirteenth Century

GENERAL IDEAS

THE aesthetics of the West of the thirteenth century is worthy of the great system of scholastic philosophy in which it is enshrined, and worthy also of an era which was a witness of considerable artistic achievement. The Gothic cathedrals arose from the soil of France, which they covered with a splendid florescence, and almost simultaneously the new harvest was spread to Germany, to England, and to Spain. Sculptors peopled these churches with statues and gave language to stones. With Giotto was born great painting; a vast surge of religious literature, popular and scholarly, was displayed in the liturgical hymns, in the *Fioretti* of St. Francis and in the *Divine Comedy* of Dante. Art, philosophy, and, one may add, the sciences developed in concentric waves and

179

made the thirteenth century one of the most interesting in the history of civilization.[1]

The prodigious success of philosophy brought with it a vigorous study of the aesthetic problem. Unfortunately the turn of the mind of the time did not attract the attention of the philosophers to the numerous works of art which were multiplying around them and which would have furnished them with incomparable objects of observation. Contemporaries of the artistic apogee, they are too near to the facts to understand their value. This is why the thinkers of the thirteenth century who reasoned about everything did not reason enough about the human activity which produces epics, cathedrals, stained-glass windows, and statues of surpassing beauty.

This is to be regretted even more because their general theories of metaphysics and their psychology of the beautiful apply excellently to artistic beauty. These theories form a perfect whole, a true system, but careful investigation is needed in order to discover it. In fact, the thirteenth century has not, any more than antiquity, taken the trouble to reassemble its aesthetic doctrines into special treatises or into thoroughgoing didactic works. Even the opusculum *De pulchro* has not this character. The doctrines concerning beauty have to be ferreted out of extensive writings on more general subjects. Thus it is with the little work which was long attributed to Thomas Aquinas [2] and which belongs to an unpublished

---

[1] See our *Civilization and Philosophy in the Middle Ages* (Princeton University Press, 1922), chaps. 5 f.

[2] Published under his name by Uccelli in 1867.

commentary of Albert the Great on the treatise *De divinis nominibus* of the Pseudo-Areopagite. Such is the case with that other of Ulrich Engelberti, a favorite pupil of Albert, which the latter incorporated into the *Summa de bono*.[3] It is necessary to bring all these theories together from writings on other matters, to gather scattered ideas and to coordinate and harmonize them with other philosophic doctrines.

To this first difficulty another is added: the aesthetic thought of the writers of the thirteenth century develops in part under the form of commentaries. They comment on the treatise of St. Augustine and on the writings of Pseudo-Dionysius, notably the treatise on the Divine Names which, after being neglected for four hundred years, becomes the object of general admiration. Now the medieval commentary is a very deceptive document; for it was the custom of an author to transmit his own personal doctrines by putting them under the patronage of a well-known name. Thus is found there a mixture of original ideas and of borrowed ones, a procedure characteristic of the time and one which in subsequent centuries proved baffling to the historian.

Apart from St. Augustine and the Pseudo-Dionysius, the Scholastics knew nothing, it can be safely stated, of the works left by the Greeks. The text of Aristotle's *Poetics* was unknown to them, even in a Latin translation; and the fragments in their possession came from a faulty commentary of Averroes, translated then recently from the Arabic by the

[3] Bk. II, tract. 3, chap. 4, *De pulchro*. Published with an excellent study by Grabmann, *Des Ulrich Engelberti von Strassburg, O. P.* (d. 1277) *Abhandlung De pulchro*, 1925.

German Hermann (d. 1272), who sets forth in only an imperfect way the thoughts of the Master. As for the *Enneads* of Plotinus, they were completely unknown in the thirteenth century.

NATURE AND ART

Following the examples of the Fathers, the writers of the thirteenth century speak in enthusiastic terms of the beauty of the universe. Each entity has its own proper place there and seeks its end. From the convergence of particular finalities results the universal order. God, the Author, is the guaranty of perpetuity. He is the universal attraction, the love which puts in motion the sun and the stars. This brings to our mind the thought of Dante's *Paradiso: L'amor che muove il sole e l'altre stelle.*

The *De pulchro* of Engelberti exclaims in enthusiastic terms on the beauty of the visible creation. "Over and above the beauty of individual things there is a special beauty of the universe, and it results from the fulfillment of a supreme beauty of the world, constituted of all the particular forms of beauty." And since even in the realms above it is not possible to have perfection and beauty greater than God's, all parts of the universe are so made that nothing can be better adapted to its utility or be more beautiful in its kind. Whence it follows that the beauty of the universe is incapable of either increase or diminution, for every loss in one part is compensated for by an increase in another; no decrease in quality, for evils but bring out the beauty of the good; none in quantity, because the disappearance of some things causes the appearance of others, and the ugliness of a fault is made up for by the beauty a just chastisement confers.[4]

"The universe," writes St. Bonaventure, "is similar to a magnificent song which unfolds its marvelous harmony, parts succeeding one another so that all things are ordered in view of their end." [5] "It is comparable," says Duns Scotus, "to a most beautiful tree, of which mortal creatures are the foliage and the branches, rational souls are the flowers, and the angels are the fruits." [6] In interpreting nature as a symbolic poem, philosophers formulate into a theory the inspirational ideas of the *Fioretti* and the *Canticle of the Sun*.

The philosophy of art occupies little space. One readily recalls the Aristotelian thesis that the work of art imitates nature. An anonymous author of the twelfth century, inspired by Aristotle, has recourse to a subterfuge in order to explain the principle of imitation in the industrial and architectural arts. He declares that mountains are the models of houses, and the plumage of the bird the exemplars of our garments.[7]

Thomas Aquinas devotes to "art" two articles in the *Summa theologica,* where he explains how art and prudence are to be distinguished.[8] The artificer of whom he speaks is

[4] Ed. Grabmann, pp. 83 f.

[5] *Commentaries on the Sentences,* I, 787 (Quarracchi edition).

[6] *De rerum principio,* q.8, a.4. This writing has been falsely attributed to Duns Scotus but is before his time. See our *Hist. de la philosophie médiévale* (ed. 1936), II, 334.

[7] Bamberg Codex on the classification of the sciences (twelfth century). Grabmann, *Geschichte der Scholastischen Methode,* II, 38.

[8] Ia IIae, q.57, a.3, 4.

as much an artisan as an artist. St. Thomas does not make any distinction between the fine arts and the industrial; or rather he is inspired by the medieval theory, in regular practice by the guilds, that every exterior production of man is capable of manifesting beauty. Art is nothing other than the right conception which directs the making of things. More briefly: *Ars est recta ratio factibilium*. Art, it is interesting to note, takes its place among the virtues under the direction of the practical reason. He who applies himself to it acquires a facility for fashioning material things, a permanent disposition making for his own perfection. While the virtue of prudence demands rectitude of the will, the virtue of art is independent of it. *Aliquis habitus habet rationem virtutis ex hoc solum quod facit facultatem boni operis—ars autem facit solum facultatem boni operis.*

The whole scholastic theory of habits is applicable to the virtue of art, and it contains in germ a program of artistic education: art ought to be cultivated like every other virtue. Its formation can involve the intervention of a master, the role of a trade union, and the influence of the traditions of a school.

One may recognize an artistic implication in the reflection which, among others, St. Bonaventure borrows from Aristotle without thoroughly fathoming its meaning: it is that a beautiful imitation can be made of an ugly thing; for example, a beautiful representation of an ugly devil (*quemadmodum dicitur imago diaboli pulchra, quando bene representat foeditatem diaboli*).⁹ A remarkable idea of art, worthy of

⁹ *Commentary on the Sentences of Peter Lombard,* I, dist. 31, part 2, a.1, q.3.

note, is contained in a verse of Dante to which we have referred elsewhere: Art is the grandson of God. The poet-philosopher who reserves a place of honor for the artist speaks of art with enthusiasm.

If the philosophers by profession (Aquinas, Bonaventure, Duns Scotus) do not enlarge upon the beauty of art, nor even on that of nature, they establish by way of compensation a general doctrine of beauty which we will try to present clearly.

Metaphysical Prolegomena

To get to the meaning of their language a few prefatory notions of scholastic metaphysics are necessary.[10] The being of corporeal nature is a reality which suffices to sustain itself as an impenetrable and independent individuality, *substantia prima*. The sensible universe is only an assemblage of individualities: men, horses, oaks, rosebushes, organisms of all kinds with a yet greater multitude of particles of inorganic matter called atoms, molecules, ions, electrons—the names matter little—and there are myriads of them. Placed in its individuality, each substance (for example, such a man, such an oak tree) is also in a species among individuals of its kind. It is indebted for this fixity of nature to the constitutive element which precisely confers on it this perfection of being self-sufficient. This it is which makes such a man, such an oak tree, what it is; and for that reason it is called the substantial form. The form is what confers on the substance its funda-

[10] See our *Initiation à la philosophie thomiste,* 1932, chaps. 4 and 5.

mental unity; and thus, because of it, all that is in the being is undivided.

But alongside this manner of being a substantial and fundamental thing, a number of adventitious realities are added to the reality of the substance in order to determine it and to exist with its existence. Besides extension, the primary attribute of body, let us mention among these "accidental" realities or superadded things, expended activity or received action, the exterior form or figure of the extended body: two types of realities which the work of art expresses with a marked predilection, and which are at the same time the most recognizable indication of the species and of the individuality. A disposition of the trunk and the splendor of the crown give to the oak a characteristic which is not constitutive of its substantiality, but is a kind of secondary being, an "accidental form." It is the same with the gesture of a wrestler, with an indication of physical or moral suffering, of a simple attitude of the human body.

Nature produces only individual substances: the Scholastics observe with Aristotle that it engenders neither houses nor temples. But it gathers into a mass individual substances: a forest, a mountain, a landscape are some of the aggregations of thousands or millions of substances, and each one enters there in its proper substantial form. However, there results from such an assemblage a sort of secondary being, and the same can be said of aggregates of substances assembled by man when he constructs edifices, paints canvases, or sculptures statues: the same accidental form covers a number of substantial forms.

These metaphysical contributions are an Aristotelian inspiration; but the theory of the form, which it is necessary for us to retain principally, receives from the western Scholastics of the thirteenth century a considerable expansion, and from several points of view it is original. The resulting aesthetic will be engrafted on the Aristotelian branch, and from it will arise new buds.

When does beauty cover with its adornment the things of nature and the works of men? Of what does it consist? The Scholastic answers: "Beauty lies in things; it is a refulgence in them which stimulates, or may stimulate, in a consciousness a characteristic impression." More briefly: "Beauty is a reciprocal act between the object and the subject: it is a result of an intimate correspondence of one with the other." Let us analyze these formulas in order to remove their obscurity and esoteric nature. Clear ideas can be made to emerge from them.

Beauty, Form, and Unity

Let us turn first to the object, to the external reality: order and its elements are constitutive of beauty. *"Commensuratio partium elegans,"* says Albert the Great; [11] *"aequalitas numerosa,"* adds Bonaventure; [12] *"debita proportio,"* writes St. Thomas. [13] The idea of order and of its constituents yields

[11] *Summa theol.,* q.26, m.1, a.2, p. 3.
[12] *Luminaria ecclesiae,* Sermon 6 (ed. Venice, 1858), I, 31.
[13] *Summa theol.,* Ia, q.5, a.4.

matter for minute analysis; what Thomas contributes is considerable, and we have shown the value he attaches to the multiplicity of parts, to their variety, and to their unity or the ordered plan which assembles them as a whole.

We have no need to compare the different texts in order to see that this thesis has a Platonic and Aristotelian inspiration. It is not Plotinus who furnished it. Undoubtedly some neo-Platonic ideas transmitted by Pseudo-Dionysius have enriched it by becoming a part of it, like the design on a rich tapestry, but the woof is not of Alexandrian origin. It is rather a number of doctrines borrowed from Aristotle, enlarged and introduced into a system: this is seen from the fact that the aesthetic order is placed in close relation with the form and unity of beings; and it is rendered of a piece with the idea of finality and of goodness.

The beauty of a being is the complete expression of its perfection (Plotinus, Pseudo-Dionysius); thus it is the expansion of what gives perfection and unity: the form. "As the form is the principle of the goodness of each being," writes U. Engelberti, "so it really constitutes the goodness of the thing. The nobility of the form is a light which gleams over all the parts of the entity." This brilliance of the form shines on the matter which has been proportioned to it; it is the creatural effect of the uncreated light.[14] There is no beauty in nature or in art if the unity is not clearly evident, if the parts are not organically linked or coherent. The principle of coherence will be the substantial form if beauty affects the

[14] Ed. Grabmann, pp. 74 f.

being in its essence; an accidental form if beauty constitutes some character, some manner of secondary being, or some activity. To produce a beautiful work, it is not sufficient to, let us say, make a complicated edifice, multiply the personages on a canvas, entangle a dramatic skein. All would be useless if a principle of order did not extend its royal control over each detail of the ensemble. "Beauty unifies what it touches, and it can do this by means of the form of the being which it sets in relief. . . . In the measure to which the form shines forth in the material parts, the whole is beautiful, and it owes its beauty to that function which it possesses of affecting a unity." [15]

Aristotle, who created the metaphysics of form, does not establish its relation to beauty. Plotinus does this, however; but, as he fails to ascribe due reality to a sensible being, the form is only a shadow of the real. The Scholastics reintegrate the real in the corporeal, and hence men, animals, plants, canvases, statues, dramas, and temples are beautiful from a beauty which is as properly theirs as the form which is immanent in them.

BEAUTY AND FINALITY

But why are the proportions of a thing of nature or of art what they are, and not something else? Because they realize their end, and the end of a being determines its nature. Per-

---

[15] "Pulchrum congregat omnia, et hoc habet ex parte formae cujus respendentia facit pulchrum . . . secundum autem quod (forma) resplendet super partes materiae, sic est pulchrum habens rationem congregandi." Albert the Great, *De pulchro*, p. 29.

fection and consequently form and its beauty are functions of finality. The aesthetic proportion is not any random one; but that which is suitable to the being. A being is beautiful when it is as it should be.

In regard to the plastic beauty of the human body, Thomas Aquinas remarks that the aesthetic disposition of its members, of the feet and of the hands, for example, is ordered to their functions. *"Si vero accipiantur membra ut manus et pes et hujusmodi, earum dispositio naturae conveniens est pulchrido."* [16] Elsewhere he describes in suggestive terms the image under which we should represent Christ, the most beautiful of the children of men, and it may be asked whether the saint had not his eyes fixed on the *Beau Dieu d'Amiens* or on some other statue of the Savior which the Gothic artists were sculpturing on the portals of the Cathedral at the moment when he himself was in the full flower of his literary production. "The beauty of one person is not that of another; and Christ possessed the beauty fitting to the state and dignity of His person. We must not represent Christ as a man with blond hair and florid countenance; that would not be suitable to Him. He possessed in a high degree a corporeal beauty which revealed His nature, His excellence, and the charm which one experienced when looking at Him. A ray of divinity evident to all lit up His features." [17]

Albert the Great believed that the body of the Blessed

---

[16] *Summa theol.,* Ia IIae, q. 54, a. 1. In scholastic language, nature is the essence of the being considered as the source of activities, directed to the end toward which these activities tend.

[17] *In Davidem,* Ps. 44:2.

Virgin manifested the three elements which constitute corporeal beauty: *elegans atque conveniens corporis magnitudo, membrorum proportionata formatio, boni et lucidi coloris perfusio.* A Dominican who came under his influence, John Balbus of Genoa, wrote a few pages on the beauty of Mary's countenance, *De splendore vultus B. Mariae.* Following James de Voragine, author of the *Golden Legend,* he sees her beauty as constituted of three colors: the black of her hair, the white of her body, and the rose-tint of her complexion. These are symbolic of her humility, her virginity, and her charity respectively.[18]

If the constitition of being is based on its finality, this finality is not necessarily the object of the aesthetic perception. We are concerned here with the metaphysical foundations of beauty. Like the foundations of an edifice, they support it even when they have not the appearance of doing so. The philosopher looks for these bases and examines their worth. The one who seeks the enjoyment of beauty is not interested in them and excludes them from his contemplation. His concern is only with those works whose sole reason for existence is their beauty.

BEAUTY AND GOODNESS

A considerable number of scholastic theories identify the beautiful with the good. "The beautiful and the good are the same," writes Pseudo-Dionysius. "All things incline with equal force toward the one and the other, no object having

[18] Grabmann, *op. cit.,* p. 17.

anything in it which does not participate in the one and the other." This text and others open the way to important discussions in which may be recognized the Greek preoccupation, but whose exact restatement will not be undertaken here.

A Thomistic formula, rich and concise, sums up this mixture of the ancient and the new: "Beauty and goodness are identical if one considers them in respect to being, which is beautiful and good. But they are not the same if one considers their relationship to the subject for whom it is beautiful and good." [19]

Every being is good, that is, every being has a natural tendency toward an end which is its good; it seeks this end and is adapted to it; the acquisition of this end or this good perfects it; the being is good in itself. In fact, the unleashing of a being's activities would not have sufficient reason if it did not result for the being itself in an increase of its reality. To regard only this aspect of reality or perfection, being and the good are convertible; both depend on a substantial form or on the primordial constituent of being. The good is being with an inclination, a term. Eliminate this inclination, and you withdraw the idea of goodness from that which diversifies the idea of being.

Therefore the beauty of a being is its perfection and the realization of its form. But this perfection must be perceived by someone, it must engender in a subject endowed with intellectual power the pleasure of contemplation. Eliminate

[19] *Summa theol.,* Ia, q.5, a.4.

this relation with a knowing subject, and you withdraw the idea of beauty from what distinguishes it from the idea of being.

Let us summarize. Perfection and being are absolute notions: goodness and beauty are relative ideas, implying a relation with an appetition or with the pleasure of knowing.

From this result the two principal differences between the Greek theory of the identity of the beautiful and the good, and the Scholastic doctrine of their resemblances and their differences. On the one hand the objective identification of the beautiful with the good admits a restriction: goodness exceeds beauty in extension. All beings are good: their internal finality draws them toward a goal in a knowing or an unknowing manner. All are not beautiful, for there are some so banal that they leave indifferent the subject who considers them: the poverty of the ontological elements does not arouse the aesthetic interest.[20] For that reason an act morally good is not necessarily beautiful. Such are the commonplace occupations of life, which are morally good without being what is designated as beautiful.

From another point of view the identification of the beautiful with the good admits a wider extension. Plato and Aristotle apply it only to the moral order, but the Scholastics extended it to the physical world, where determinism reigns. It remains true, however, that the distinction between the two ideas of goodness and beauty appears with the greatest

[20] We do not think that the Scholastics regarded beauty as a transcendental (quod transcendit omne genus).

clearness when one transfers it to the field of human action. An act of heroism is at the same time both beautiful and good. The passer-by who at the risk of his own life plunges into the water to save a person drowning performs a good action, for devotion to the neighbor is one of these supreme forms of morality which make man great in his own eyes and are for him a source of merit. At the same time this rescuing is a beautiful action, not in its material circumstances which render the spectacle distressing, but in its moral significance, and this the witnesses of a drama will not fail to recognize. Now it is interesting to note that the act is good for the one who performs it, and beautiful for the one who views it. The hero of a drama will withdraw from the scene with a legitimate feeling of internal satisfaction, but he will not admire his own conduct from the standpoint of the aesthetic. Ontologically the moral act is the same act in its goodness as in its beauty; it takes on different aspects only as we relate it first to a subject who receives from it greatness and merit, and then to one who enjoys the spectacle of their harmonious combination.

Thus it is in the impression produced in the knowing being that the notion of beauty is perfected. The psychological effects of the beautiful are inseparable from its ontological reality. Their study introduces us to a new aspect of the question.

CHAPTER XIV

The Aesthetics of the Thirteenth Century: Psychological Problems

INTELLECTUALISM

THE Scholastic of the thirteenth century, fully awake to the psychological problem, gives ample attention to the impression that beauty makes. In the nature of this impression and in its factors we shall note, at the outset, a leaning toward the Greek doctrines to which the Aristotelian and Platonic traditions gave a definite consistency: the aesthetic activity is an activity of perception; it is achieved in an enjoyment which is at the same time a stimulus and likewise a recompense.

Numerous and concordant texts establish the principle that beauty is an affair of knowledge; that it is nourished by visual and auditory sensations, by intellectual images and ideas; and that it interests our whole perceptive being. "The beautiful has to do with the power of knowing; for we call a thing beautiful the knowledge of which pleases us." [1] Nevertheless the intervention of the senses, of the imagination, of the intellect, is not translated by separate psychic efforts independent one of the other, like the stalks of wheat bound together in a sheaf. A central and primordial act penetrates the whole operation and imprints on it an aesthetic character: it is an abstraction or a royal act of the mind.[2] Complementary sensations and images are placed at the service of the intellect, which perceives in the rich data the principle or reason of order, and in one swift act grasps the unity of the thing of nature or of the work of art. *Cognitio ordinis est solius intellectus.* "Of all the animals only man takes pleasure in the knowledge of sensible bodies," says Thomas Aquinas, "for the knowledge alone, that is, for their beauty." [3]

Several of those theories are familiar and therefore we can take them up again in abridged form. Intellectualism is the foundation stone of Thomism, in the sense that the implications of this doctrine, left in the shadow by Aristotle and Plotinus, are there clearly defined. One of these brings to light an unsolved problem in the great medieval philosophy and touches on a difficulty which runs through the whole of its ideology. Since sensation and intellect concur in the per-

---

[1] "Pulchrum respicit vim cognoscitivam; pulchra enim dicuntur quae visa placent." St. Thomas, *Summa theol.,* Ia, q.5, a.4. The word *"visa"* is here taken in a general sense.

[2] In scholastic language one would say that the act of intellection is the formal element of the aesthetic perception, the one that gives the whole its specific character.

[3] Ia, q.39, a.3, ad 3.

ception of a work of art, this perception has for its object "a harmony of abstract ideas in the particular."

There is here no difficulty as to the sensations, for their proper domain is that of figures, of colors, of lines, of sounds, where each is particular and individual. But what are we to say of the intellect? Is not its natural and spontaneous function that of abstracting the real from whatever it comes into contact with; that is to say, to strip clear the essence by its grasp of all that binds it to the individual? Can it contemplate the grace, the majesty, the smile in a Madonna well sculptured, in such a manner as to comprehend the indissoluble union established by the artist between the general ideas and their aesthetic development? Is the intellectual intuition of the particular possible, having been given the Thomistic ideology?

Whatever one thinks of the solution that Thomas Aquinas proposes and that we have not discussed here, the intuition of the abstract in the individual, artistic or other, is for the human intellect an inferior operation and less perfect than the act of abstraction exercised for itself and for the love of truth. There, I think, is the reason for the little attention and for the low esteem that the Thomist grants to the perception of art. For Aristotle, poetry is less philosophical than history. Thomas Aquinas has added that art is less philosophical than science. Art does not attain directly to the abstract, the scientific for itself, since it embodies it in sensible forms and causes it to shine out in the individual. In that respect it is inferior to science. Because he was so thoroughly a scientist,

Thomas Aquinas places beauty on an inferior plane. This lover of knowledge is influenced by general classifications and vast syntheses, like the century to which he belongs.

The contemplation of natural and artistic beauty is accompanied by a serene love and a penetrating delight. It is again in conformity with their intellectual theory that the Scholastics interpret both the one and the other. The human reason delights in perfection and beauty, because it is itself perfection and beauty; the soul recognizes itself therein; it inclines toward that which resembles it. The love of the beautiful is disinterested, free from the desire of possessing a thing otherwise than to contemplate it. Thus beauty is not that which delights, but that whose apprehension or perception produces joy. "It is said that an object is good when it is pleasing to the appetitive faculty; but it is beautiful when the mere knowledge of it delights." [4] It should be noted well that the enjoyment of beauty, like every enjoyment and every emotion, has its foundation in the appetite of which it is a modality. This is the application of a thesis of scholastic psychology that we do not intend to expound here: the desire rises from the appetite as does also the satisfaction that follows from the accomplished desire and the enjoyment which results from it. [5]

[4] "Et sic patet quod pulcrum addit supra bonum quemdam ordinem ad vim cognoscitivam; ita quod bonum dicatur id quod simpliciter complacet appetitui, pulcrum autem dicatur id cujus apprehensio placet." Ia IIae, q.27, a.1.

[5] "Pulcritudo non habet rationem acceptibilis, nisi inquantum induit rationem boni; sic enim et verum appetibile est; sed secundum rationem propriam habet claritatem." In Lib. I Sent., dist. 31, q.2. "Cum enim bonum sit quod omnia appetunt, de ratione boni est quod in eo quietetur appetitus. Sed ad rationem pulcri pertinet quod in ejus aspectu seu cognitione quietetur appetitus." Ia IIae, q.27, a.1.

THEORY OF THE SPLENDOR OF BEAUTY

The perception and enjoyment which compose the aesthetic impression are not the mere accessories of beauty, epiphenomena which are produced when a human being contemplates the beautiful but to which beauty itself remains a stranger. The intimation of beauty rests in a determined adaptation of the order of things to contemplation of which this order is the food and the end. This is what is most original in the aesthetics of the Scholastics.

This correlation upholds the theory of clarity or the resplendence of the beautiful.

All that the Greeks of Platonic-Aristotelian lineage attribute to the charm of color,[6] all that the Alexandrians and Pseudo-Dionysius [7] write about light, finds itself here charted into a vaster synthesis with new meaning. To be beautiful, order must not be merely present in some way or other; it must shine out; for this end it must be proportioned to the human capacities in such a way as to arouse contemplation easily and amply. The appropriation which Aristotle points out as mere incidence [8] is here rendered obligatory; it is introduced into the idea of beauty with the same title as order and proportion; it helps to constitute it. This correlation does not result from Engelberti's relative to *lux formalis*, but it is clearly expressed by the other Scholastics.

[6] See, for example, Xenophon, *Memorabilia*, III, X; Cicero, *Tusculan Disputations*, IV, 13; St. Augustine, *Homil. in Ps. 44, Ep.* 18.

[7] Plotinus, *Enneads*, I, 6 *et passim;* St. Basil, *Hexameron*, II, 7; Pseudo-Dionysius, *Concerning the Divine Names*, IV, 4.

[8] In his theory of due proportion (*Metaph.*, III, 3; *Poetics*, VII).

Splendor says more than light and color: splendor is light
and color rendered visible, *lumen apparens, lumen mani-
festans, color nitidus*.[9] "If someone is the object of honors
and praise," writes St. Thomas, "he becomes *clarus* (famous)
in the eyes of other men."[10] The *De pulcro* says: "Light
involves merely some not excessively bright emission from a
lighted fire-place; but the beautiful requires its brilliance."[11]
"Also," concludes Duns Scotus, "clarity is a sort of resplendence, and it adds to the idea of light and color that of a manifestation. A clear light, a clear truth, and a clear idea imply
a perfect manifestation of this light, of this truth, of this
idea."[12]

Brightness is therefore to the beautiful what evidence is
to truth. It does not attach itself to a visible color only, as in
the popular Greek formula, in the discourses of Parrhasius
related by Xenophon, or in the theories of Cicero and St.
Augustine, but more especially to the things of the super-
sensible order. The spiritual beauty of man is other than
the plastic beauty of his corporeal members. "It consists in
this, that his social relations or his acts are well proportioned
and are clothed with the splendor which is given by the suprasensible brightness of his reason."[13]

On the other hand the "clarity" of the Scholastics is not

[9] St. Thomas, *Summa theol.*, IIa IIae, q. 142, a. 4; q. 180, a. 2; Ia, q. 39, a. 8.
[10] *Ibid.*, IIa IIae, q. 145, a. 8.
[11] *De pulcro*, p. 37.
[12] Commentaries on the Sentences, Bk. IV.
[13] "Et similiter pulcritudo spiritualis in hoc consistit quod conversatio homi-
nis sive actio ejus sit bene proportionata secundum spiritualem rationis claritatem." St. Thomas, *Summa theol.*, IIa IIae, q. 145, a. 2.

like the "light" of the Alexandrians, a purely metaphysical attribute independent of the knowledge we can obtain of it. As it makes the order shine out to render it visible, its bright-ness ought to be proportioned to the poor means of knowl-edge that we possess. Beauty becomes a human reality, a purely human one; the incommensurable and the incompre-hensible features of the mystical world of the Neo-Platonists is beyond beauty.

Splendor Attributed to the Form

This resplendence has to do with the form of being. Beauty is called splendor of form, substantial or accidental, dominat-ing the proportional and determined parts of matter.[14] This is a doctrine which harmonizes with the master theories of metaphysics and ideology. The form, indeed, is at the same time the root of the perfection proper to each being, the pivot of its unity, and the principle of its intelligibility. As comprehender of being, the intellect is the receiver of the form which is a primordial constituent of a being. Hence all that concerns beauty is related to the form. *"Quia cognitio fit per assimilationem, assimilatio autem respicit formam, pulcrum proprie pertinet ad rationem causae formalis."* [15] The more resplendent the form is, the easier and fuller will be the impression made; this is the price of beauty. It will be the substantial form which will shine forth in a thing of nature, an accomplished type of its species. It will also

[14] Albert the Great, *De pulcro*, p. 29.
[15] St. Thomas, *Summa theol.*, Ia, q.5, a.4.

be a secondary or accidental form, as a shape or an activity. *Notio pulcri, in universali consistit in resplendentia formae super partes materiae proportionatas vel super diversas vires vel actiones.*[16]

This would have been the point at which to begin a philosophy of art. What does the artist do, if not deposit in the sensible materials the splendor of a principle of unity, liberally chosen from the innumerable *formae accidentales* into which this material may be fashioned? Builders of cathedrals and sculptors make radiant systems of lines in stones and wood, *super partes materiae proportionatas.* Painters, sculptors, and poets exercise power over physical and moral activities which often exact the collaboration of a considerable number of personages, *vel super diversas actiones,* and Gothic statues in their simple gestures suggest to the onlookers the interior life and all the resources of action with which a being is endowed, *super diversas vires.*[17] In the metaphysics of the beautiful is found enclosed a theory of art, like an ear of grain in its sheaf.

CONCLUSION

After what has preceded, a person can understand why the *debita proportio* and the *claritas* were unanimously looked upon in the thirteenth century as the essential elements of beauty: the first sums up all that beauty expresses in objects,

---

[16] Albert the Great, *De pulcro,* p. 29.
[17] The Scholastic ditinguishes between the operative powers, *vires,* and the operation resulting from them, *actio.*

the second implies the intervention of the psychological factors and the adequate relation of the object contemplated to the contemplative activity.

Medieval aesthetics is the final outgrowth of the Greek aesthetic, its logical conclusion. It blends into a concordant synthesis the Platonic-Aristotelian point of view and the point of view of Plotinus; it transcends, however, both the one and the other. This achievement is more to be appreciated from the fact that the thirteenth century knew neither the text of Aristotle's *Poetics* nor the *Enneads* of Plotinus.

CHAPTER XV

Greek Aesthetics and Medieval Aesthetics

GREEK AESTHETICS

A GENERAL characteristic dominates Greek aesthetics from the time of the early beginnings in the *Memorabilia* of Xenophon up to its efflorescence in the *Enneads* of Plotinus: beauty is an attribute of things. It envelops them; it penetrates them; this it does without our intervention, and even before we perceive it.

This objectivity is not understood in the same manner by Plato and Aristotle on the one hand, and by Plotinus and the Alexandrians on the other. The former look for beauty in the internal order of a being, or in the harmonious assemblage of various beings. For five or six centuries this doctrine had appealed strongly to the Greeks. It penetrated the Hel-

lenic mentality until Plotinus opposed it by a new thesis
which rivaled the first, but without supplanting it. Extend-
ing the spheres of beauty, the Alexandrian master wished
to discover it not only in what is ordered, and therefore com-
posite, but also in what is simple. "Every being is beautiful,"
he writes, "as every being is one, true, and good; beauty
transcends categories and genera, and order is only a means
to make it shine forth in a limited group of realities."

Objectivists, these two groups of aesthetic theories have
this trait in common, that they are forms of intellectualism.
The three giants of Greek philosophy agree in saying, for
reasons proper to each, that we grasp the beauty of things
by a knowledge superior to that which the simple sensation
furnishes. For all three this mode of knowledge is the intellective mode or abstraction. Even in the psychology of Plotinus, the securing possession of the reality-type, or of the
intelligibility of things, by means of these abstract and general ideas, remains the central act of the aesthetic life; for
direct intuition of the One is a mystic intermittent phenomenon which remains the privilege of exceptional souls.

It is in knowing beauty that we come in contact with it.
In knowing it, we enjoy being acquainted with it. Plato,
Aristotle, and Plotinus, especially the last two, have analyzed
the contents of aesthetic consciousness. Psychologists all,
they were compelled to interest themselves in the subject.
But their attention to it was only incidental and for the purpose of consigning and describing phenomena which could
not be neglected, but which add nothing to beauty. These

exist before the impression they engender and without it, in such a manner that the impression is an adventitious thing and therefore secondary. All Greek aestheticism has some metaphysical bearing.

From this fact arises the last trait to be met with in the two groups of theories, the Platonic-Aristotelian and the Plotinian: beauty of art and beauty of nature are not studied for themselves but in the function of beauty in general. No philosophy of art is distinct from metaphysics. Plato's contempt for the work of art, as well as the respect which Plotinus bestowed upon it, was dictated by the principles of their respective metaphysics; and it is of a piece with the enthusiasm of Plotinus for sensible nature.

MEDIEVAL AESTHETICS

The Platonic-Aristotelian and the Neo-Platonic aesthetics survived Greek civilization. They were collected by the Fathers of the Church, and through St. Augustine and Pseudo-Dionysius they contribute the numerous allusions of these to the formation of medieval ideas. We must turn back to the thirteenth century, the era in which Western civilization and Western philosophy produced the most savory fruits, in order to view an aesthetic elaboration worthy of arresting the attention of the historian. The philosophers of the thirteenth century revived both the Aristotelian and the Alexandrian cycle, giving both a logical embodiment of their thought. They combine the theories not in the manner of eclectics, by a procedure of juxtaposition, but by placing them in harmony with their great doctrinal system, where all is coherence and solidarity. The foundation is evident: order alone is the generator of beauty, whether it is a question of an isolated being or an assemblage of beings, a question of nature or of art. Order is the principle of perfection, of unity, of form which gives each being its individuality. A few Alexandrian ideas appear, like the ornamentation of a frame, but they take on a new meaning: the relation of the beautiful to the good, the aesthetic role of the form, the value of light, all is understood differently by Pseudo-Dionysius and Thomas of Aquin. The most original idea of the scholastic aesthetics is the placing of value on the impression which the Scholastics relate to the very essence of beauty. Beauty is not only that which is ordered, but that which by this same order is susceptible of producing in the man who perceives it the joy of contemplation. A relation of appropriation is established between the exterior reality and the impression which it should produce, and beauty exists only in such a relation. The *claritas pulcri* becomes an essential element by virtue of due proportion.

In remaining objectivist, medieval aesthetics, like that of the Greeks, gives the psychological element a primordial place, and thus beauty ceases to be a simple attribute of things. In the same way the philosophers of the Middle Ages emphasized the intellectual aspect of their doctrine, for it is through the intellect that the order of things must be understood and relished. In aesthetics, as in the other branches of their philosophy, they are the champions of the doctrine that views the force, the nobility, the source of conscious life as residing in the act of cognition.

Plato, Aristotle, Plotinus, St. Augustine, Pseudo-Dionysius, and St. Thomas Aquinas form an unbroken line. Personalities of the first order, they represent various stages in the same philosophical development; they enlighten eighteen centuries of human thinking. A chain of gold connects them. Thanks to them, "the whole line of human beings during the course of so many centuries may be considered one man, who subsists always and who learns continually." [1]

[1] Pascal, *Opuscules* (ed. Brunschvigg), p. 80.

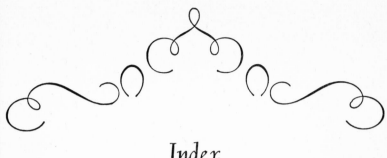

Index